Pavlov's Trout

Also by Paul Quinnett:

Darwin's Bass
Fishing Lessons
Suicide: The Forever Decision

Pavlov's Trout

The
Incompleat Psychology
of
Everyday Fishing

Paul Quinnett

Andrews McMeel
Publishing

Kansas City

Hardcover and paperback editions of this book were published in 1994 by Keokee Co. Publishing, Inc.

www.andrewsmcmeel.com

Library of Congress Cataloging-in-Publication Data
Quinnett, Paul G., 1939–
    Pavlov's trout : the incompleat psychology of everyday fishing / Paul G. Quinnett.
      p.   cm.
    ISBN 0-8362-6840-7 (ppb)
    1. Fishings. 2. Fishing—Psychological aspects.
3. Fishing—Philosophy. 4. Fishing stories. I. Title.
SH421.Q56   1998
799.1'019—dc21   98-18117
                                                   CIP

799.1—dc21
                                               98-3986
                                                 CIP

ATTENTION: SCHOOLS AND BUSINESSES

Andrews McMeel books are available at quantity discounts with bulk purchase for educational, business, or sales promotional use. For information, please write to: Special Sales Department, Andrews McMeel Publishing, 4520 Main Street, Kansas City, Missouri 64111.

Contents

Foreword

I've just come in from fishing. Caught only one, a 10-inch kokanee, but enough for my breakfast. I stayed out longer than I should have, hoping to catch at least one more, so my wife, Bun, could have a fish for her breakfast, too. I explained the reason for my tardiness, and she said that had been very thoughtful of me. One tries to be considerate.

My intention had been to spend the day writing a foreword to Paul Quinnett's latest book, *Pavlov's Trout*. Instead, I went fishing. That's something Paul would appreciate, at least if the foreword was for someone else's book. As it is, he seems to be getting a little testy. So I'd better hop to it.

Because Paul Quinnett and I are good friends, you might reasonably suspect that I would be tempted to praise his book beyond its merits. To allay such fears, I can only say, "Yes, but not that good of friends." I could easily predict, for example, that *Pavlov's Trout* will survive the test of time and become a fishing classic. Alas, I cannot in good conscience make such a prediction. All I can predict is that it will be a top contender for that title. *Pavlov's Trout* is a first-rate book.

Pavlov's Trout is an oddity among fishing books. For one thing, it's interesting. For another thing, it says absolutely nothing about how to catch fish, which may explain the first thing. What this book is about is the psychology of fishing, or perhaps the abnormal psychology of fishing. It is about Becoming and Being a fisherman.

Paul Quinnett is a psychologist. He admits it himself, so I run no risk of offending him by mentioning the fact here. He specializes in suicide, or the prevention thereof, and in fact is one of the leading experts in the world on this form of ceasing to be. I suppose that is why he spends so much time thinking about life. He is also one of the busiest human beings I know. Besides his work as a psychologist, he writes 50 or so articles a year and is usually working on a book, as well as delivering dozens of speeches around the nation. Despite this schedule, he manages to fish more than anybody I know, with the possible exception of fishing guides, another occupation, by the way, to which Paul aspires.

I first met Quinnett when he showed up at one of my writing workshops at Eastern Washington University. He said he had long dreamed of becoming a professional writer and wanted to know how to do it. I told him. He then went off and became one. I don't mean to suggest it was that easy. He probably wrote 50,000 words or more before he sold his first article. By the end of the workshop, however, he had written and sold at least a dozen articles and in addition had written most of a book, *When Self-Help Fails*, which received excellent, even rave, reviews upon publication. It was at that point that I began to study Paul Quinnett. Here was a person who had a dream of becoming something more than he was and then set out to become the dream, and became it, just like that. As I mentioned earlier, Becoming is one of the themes of *Pavlov's Trout*.

The chapter on fishing ethics is one of my favorites. I've read quite a bit about ethics over the years, mostly out of curiosity. While the authors of such works are not always tedious, they certainly qualify as spoilsports. Quinnett makes ethics not only interesting but appealing. If enough people read this chapter, ethics could even catch on. It would be nice to see the whole country swept by a wave of ethics as a result of this book. I may give them a try myself.

The title chapter, "Pavlov's Trout," is about this Dr. Pavlov who spent years tying up dogs and then ringing a bell every time he gave them a tidbit of food. After a while, the dogs started to salivate as soon as they heard the dinner bell, whether any food was present or not. Quinnett finds a most interesting connection between this experiment and fishing, one well worth the price of the book all by itself. (Or you can send me two dollars, and I'll tell you what it is.) As for Dr. Pavlov, he was never apprehended and may still be at large.

Quinnett is an existential fisherman, as becomes evident in the final chapter of the book, where he tells of seeing the death of the world fast approaching over the horizon and tries to get a few more casts in before it arrives. Fishing is at the core of his being and may even be the core. The rest of his life seems to be a support system for his fishing. His wife, Ann — a saint! — doesn't in the least seem to mind his fishing addiction and apparently even encourages it. On their typical fishing trip together, she reads happily in the car while he fishes. (So, young persons, let this be a lesson to you: Never marry a psychologist!) Paul thinks a great deal about his life, and about his death, too. He doesn't know, he says, whether he will end up in heaven or hell, but he does wonder if he should take waders.

Pavlov's Trout treads lightly and with great good humor over many serious subjects, which in some way the author always manages to connect with fishing. He is, as I have indicated, a master of connecting with fishing. Paul Quinnett is one of the finest essayists writing today, as you will discover for yourself in reading this book. Afterward, if you are a fisherman, you will know a good deal more about yourself. And if you are not a fisherman, you most certainly will want to become one.

Patrick F. McManus
Clark Fork, Idaho

Preface

This book is about the psychology of fishing. Or maybe it is a fishing expedition through human psychology in search of fishing man. Whatever it is, it was a lot of fun to write.

I've been a psychologist for the last 25 fishing seasons, but in that time, I've managed to keep one foot in the consulting office and the other in a trout stream. I've been an angler all my life. From these happy perspectives, I've learned a little about human nature, quite a bit about fishermen and become almost an expert on the taking of wild cutthroat trout.

Whatever else this book is, it is not a lot of science. Rather, my aim is, like Mr. Izaak Walton before me, to provide some "profit or pleasure . . . mixt with some innocent mirth."

All patients herein described have been thoroughly disguised to protect their confidentiality. What research is mentioned was honestly borrowed from real scientists who, slaving away in their labs instead of fishing, give us new ideas to enhance our thinking about human nature. Their names and books are mentioned in the text for those who may wish to take the bait and run with it.

Speaking of bait and ideas and such, let me end the beginning with the opening stanza of John Donne's *The Baite*.

Come live with me, and bee my love,
and wee will some new pleasures prove
of golden sands, and christall brookes,
with silken line, and silver hookes.

Good reading.

Paul Quinnett
Cheney, Washington

Many men go fishing all their lives without knowing that it is not fish they are after.

— Henry David Thoreau

The universe is full of magical
things, patiently waiting for our
wits to grow sharper.

— Eden Phillpotts

The Grass Pickerel and Other
Motivational Mysteries

Many sunny Junes ago on one of my exploratory fishing rambles I discovered a stream at the bottom of a deep coulee cut by the great floods that carved the ancient lava flows of eastern Washington into the canyons and sinks and lake beds that make this land so rugged and remarkable. Thinking there might be fish in this hidden place, I grabbed a spinning rod, stuck a small box of lures and hooks in my shirt pocket, and scrambled down a talus slope to see what I might see.

The French Mepps people make one of the finest search-and-find spinners ever invented. After only a couple of casts with their No. 2 brass blade into the head of a long, deep pool, I had a pretty good rainbow trout dancing. A couple of casts later I hooked a bulldog fighter of a largemouth bass; not very big, but spunky. I hooked a small cutthroat. After seeing the fin of a carp slip by, I switched to a hook and bobber, grubbed a worm from the stream bank, and promptly caught a brown bullhead. Then a pumpkinseed. Then a perch. I was studying a pod of carp as they swept by when, again, my bobber dived and I set the hook, only to reel in a fish I had never seen before.

Had I stumbled into God's personal aquarium?

I took a long study of the fish, released it, and got right back to fishing. At the rate I was going, my next cast might land me a tuna — and I'm especially fond of tuna.

At home later, I dug out A. J. McClane's *New Standard Fishing Encyclopedia*, and found the mystery fish on page 789: a grass pickerel, old *Esox americanus vermiculatus*. It is almost identical to the redfin pickerel, and both are called "little pickerel." They are the smallest members of the pike family, rarely growing larger than 14 or 15 inches. The one that fell for my worm was about eight inches long.

Now the mystery deepened. According to McClane, the redfin pickerel is native to the Atlantic drainage, while the grass pickerel, a western cousin, is found in the Great Lakes and Mississippi drainage. The grass was originally and naturally dispersed throughout Lake Ontario and Lake Erie, into Pennsylvania, eastern Kentucky, Tennessee, and into Alabama. From there, it was apparently carried by fishermen into states like Ohio, Indiana, Michigan, Illinois and even Texas. But Washington State?

Since pickerel don't walk, a fisherman must have had a hand in my puzzle. Fishermen have always been Johnny Pumpkinseeds. They scatter their favorite fishes along the waterways they travel. Westward-moving Americans brought their favorite fishes with them in rain barrels lashed to the sides of covered wagons. Finding the great rivers and streams of the Himalayas devoid of trout, British colonists stocked the cold waters with their favorite species and began teaching Indians the art of fly tying.

In McClane's last paragraph on the little pickerel my mystery was solved. He notes, "There was an unrecorded introduction of the grass pickerel at some unknown time into the northeast portion of the state of Washington."

Bingo!

Who brought the fish here when, why and by what means are all questions that some super sleuth might choose to puzzle out. Personally, I wonder how the little buggers go with a dash of Dijon mustard.

The point of my story is that we fishermen love a mystery, and maybe more than most. We love what *might* lie under a watery surface, or in the depths of a deep pool, or just beyond a barrier reef.

It is, I think, this unquenchable curiosity that makes our species unique. It is this wondering, this insatiable thirst to explore beyond our reach, that leads us, with nothing more than hook and line, to reconnoiter where we cannot go and canvass what we cannot see.

And then, there is hope.

Curiosity and Hope

The Japanese say, "It is better to travel hopefully than to arrive." This could be rewritten for fishermen, "It is better to fish hopefully than to catch fish."

Some young anglers might disagree, but no old fisherman would. Fishing is hope experienced.

When it comes to the human spirit, hope is all. Without hope, there is no yearning, no desire for a better tomorrow, and no belief that the next cast will bring the big strike. Without hope, there is no wonder, no mystery and no reason to bother traveling at all.

He hasn't met you Stvie

Fishermen are an optimistic lot . . . chronically optimistic . . . and to be optimistic in a slow bite is to thrive on hope alone. When asked, "How can you fish all day without a hit?" the true fisherman replies, "Hold it! I think I felt something." When the line again goes slack, he says, "He'll be back!" This is hope defined.

Catching a fish is hope affirmed.

The part of a fishing trip that lifts the heart with excitement is the going out; the hike into the lake over the mountain, the boat ride to the far shoal, the long drive through the night to a new river. We travel hopefully. It doesn't matter what disappointments might lie ahead. We travel toward a promise in high spirits. Nothing and no one can subtract from this feeling of hope brimming over.

Fishing tackle manufacturers do not sell things that catch fish. They sell hope, and they should. Fishing is chancy and mysterious, and a challenge all the days of a man's life. Skill is important. Luck and weather and hope are more important, and of these, hope is the key. Without hope, the fisherman would soon quit his day, his purpose for Being.

A line in the water is hope extended.

I have fished with people who say, after an hour of no luck, "Ah, let's give it up. This is hopeless." If they reel in and put their rod down to pout, I make a note never to go fishing with them again. Hopelessness, like hope, is contagious.

Hopelessness is pessimistic and dour. Hope is powerful and filled with self-confidence. Good anglers practice the power of positive thinking. They fish hard. They fish long. They never stop casting. They fish from dawn till dusk, and into the night. They fish as if every cast will draw a strike. They troll on hour after hour without a hit. Without hope, they would quit — perhaps forever.

To live long and fish well, a fisherman must learn to travel hopefully.

Despite all the bad news, the threats to our waters and fishes, and to the places we so love and need, we fishermen have a bright future. We have come a long way in the last 50 years. We have gotten a little smarter, a little bolder in our views and actions, and we have a deeper grasp of the things that matter in the great web of life. We are learning to travel hopefully, to honor the fish we love and the places in which the fishes live. We are solving some of the mysteries, only to find more mysteries. Successful fishermen are curious, drawn to a mystery, and hopeful.

And, they are motivated, powerfully motivated, by something more than just catching fish.

The Angler's Angle

It has been said that motivation is the black box of modern psychology. The term "motivation" is a puzzle. It describes everything, but explains nothing.

If a nesting largemouth bass savagely strikes a passing spinner bait, it may have been *motivated* to attack an enemy.

What *motivates* a trout to rise to one dry fly, but not another?

If a creature goes fishing every Saturday, for trout or largemouth bass, it must be *motivated* to do so.

What does "motivated" mean? Prompted? Actuated? Incited? Provoked? Aroused? Excited? Triggered? Inflamed? Encouraged? Lured? Driven by instinct? Drawn? Motivated?

You see how it goes.

Psychologists are not supposed to engage in this sort of circular logic. Heat, rather than light, is the chief product. Nor are psychologists supposed to explain one unhelpful word with another. Motivation is as elusive as the Loch Ness monster. No one has ever seen a motive, touched a motive, weighed a motive, or filmed a motive. And they never will.

Referred to as a "psychological construct" by Ph.D.s with too much time on their hands, motivation is just an airy word someone dreamed up to explain one of those knotty, unyielding mysteries of life.

Mother to son just back from college: "Why are you going fishing instead of mowing the lawn?"

Son: "I feel a deep and abiding motivation to, that's why."

Mother: "Well, as long as you're motivated, it's okay. Is that one of those big words you learned in college?"

Pity the poor picked-on professors who study motivation in futile attempts to account for the "whys" of behavior — in fish, white rats or humans. For example, consider how complex the answers might be to the following fishing questions.

Do anglers angle because they're hungry?

They usually pack a lunch, so there must be other reasons.

Do fishermen angle because they want to avoid trimming the hedges?

Maybe.

Do they angle because they love to be out in nature?

Possibly, but they can get a nature fix elsewhere.

Do they angle because it's fun?

Probably. But sometimes it isn't fun. Sometimes it's cold and wet and miserable.

Do they angle because they have a built-in fishing motive that, like the golf motive, drives them to it?

Huh?

And, here's an academic question for a researcher without enough to do. If fishing is so darned innocent, why do they call it *angling*? Doesn't "angle" mean a kind of approach, a scheme, a manipulation, a way to get something you want without letting anyone know what you're up to?

A related academic question: If angle worms are angled, how come the ones I've seen wriggle like a snake?

The "Why" Question

One of the reasons I got into psychology in the first place is that I am constantly incited to fits of thinking by the peskiest question of all. Why?

The why question appears in the language of human beings around age two and is never fully and finally answered. Parents try, and fail. So do schools, teachers and institutions of higher learning.

"Why?" is the most common question asked by two- and three-year-olds, which may be *why* so many parents become so frustrated with their little ones during this developmental phase. When two of my children were going through the "why" stage, I was an instructor in developmental psychology. I was fully aware of the negative impact on intellectual development that occurs if you shut a kid down or punish him or her for asking the most natural question in the world. I nearly ended up on medication. However, when grown-ups try mightily to answer the "why" question, and encourage more whys, toddlers go on asking until they win a Nobel Prize, or retire as astrophysicists, successful novelists or even psychologists.

Not getting answers to "Why?" leads kids to stop asking, and contributes to the death of their curiosity and hope, perhaps even condemning them to a life of boredom and watching daytime television.

Fishermen who keep coming up with one more why question become fish biologists, or ichthyologists, or ecologists, or design engineers for fishing lure manufacturers. The truly cursed become inventors of new fly patterns.

Whatever finally comes of asking the why question, the important thing is never to stop asking. If you stop asking, you are likely to end up with some peculiar beliefs.

The world is flat, for example.

The sun moves around the earth.

Trout don't bite on a full moon.

Another big reason I got into psychology on the clinical side was to try to understand what motivated me; why I did some of the screwy things I did. Following the ancient advice, "Physician, heal thyself," and in keeping with the psychologist's code of specializing in our own defect, I have taken pains to study the whys and wherefores of my fishing behavior. I will share what small gains I have made down the path toward an answer.

The Search for the Grass Pickerel

Each of us still above ground has an innate sense of wonder, a curiosity; a need to know what lies over the next hill, beyond the meadow, in the ocean deep, at the bottom of the brook and past the Milky Way. If we don't have this sense of excitement at the possibilities beyond our reach, we're probably brain dead, waiting for someone to come and kick dirt over us.

Restlessness is as fundamental to the human spirit as breath is to life, and fishermen, if they keep fishing, and especially if they continue to feel that little tight spot in their chests at the prospect of new water and fishes yet unknown, know exactly what I'm talking about.

Return for a moment to that bluff overlooking the hidden stream where I caught the grass pickerel. Why was I out there in the first place? Certainly there were better known and more reliable places to catch fish that day. It wasn't as if there weren't other things to do, like see a movie, wash the truck, read a book, have lunch with my wife, volunteer time in a worthy cause, write my congressman or, on the theory that desire to experience is nearly as good as the experience itself, tie trout flies.

There are always things to do in life, things that need attention, things to react to. But *reacting to* life is different than *acting on* life. One is passive and believed necessary. The other is creative and often unnecessary; or appears to be so to those without a sense of wonder.

Fishermen, by my measure of them, are largely actors *on* life, not reactors *to* life. This difference in how to be in this world is never insignificant, especially if you believe it is passion that quickens life, expands the time allotted to us, and fills every new day with the promise of discovery.

Notes from the Lab

Researchers uniformly report newborn fishermen have a powerful, intrinsic need to reach out, grab hold of something and stick it in their mouths. This allows otherwise immobile, crib-bound, helpless infants the opportunity to explore, understand and manage the only environment available to them.

This is how infants learn. Everything and anything they can lay their hands on, they look at, smell, taste and manipulate with their pudgy little fingers. Having gained mastery over it and decided "it is not me," they toss it aside and look for something new and novel to stick in their mouth.

Study the faces of babies and listen to their gurgles and coos. Mastering their little world seems to bring them enjoyment and pleasure. All human infants have this exploratory drive, called mastery-motivation.

Curiosity and a need to explore, understand and master the environment is as much a part of being human beings as having fingers and feet, toes and thumbs. And, we have fingers and thumbs to bait hooks and tie flies, and feet and toes to carry us with balance and grace to the streams and ponds we hope to explore for fishes to master. Why would a fisherman come otherwise equipped?

As we grow up we continue to explore and master more and more of our environment and, in the process, get more and more of our "why" questions answered. Like building blocks, we pile each new experience atop an older one until, one day, we are all grown up, have fished all the water within a day's drive, can build our own bass rods, patch our own waders, and are wondering what's left we haven't already done twice. We even answer "why" questions for younger fishermen.

Growing a little bored, we ask ourselves what sort of fish swim in the lakes beyond the mountain range. Or another 10 miles out on the ocean? Or down in Mexico? Before we know it, we're off on new adventures. When we're old, we want to say of the great fishing holes, "Been there. Done that. Bought the shirt."

As much as slow death, fishermen abhor boredom, which is why I chanced to hike down into the canyon to fish the secret stream where I caught the grass pickerel and also why I have spent the better part of my adult life helping people puzzle out their mysteries.

I am rarely bored. If anything, I feel shortchanged at having been allotted but a single lifetime. One is hardly sufficient time to wet a line in a tenth of the good water west of the Rocky Mountains, let alone all over this wonderfully watery planet, even if I could discount silly prior obligations like a job and family.

Mysteries of the Fishes

Catching the grass pickerel did not solve a mystery, it started one. This is good, when you consider that it is our nature to grasp hold of new things, study them, and ask questions so that we can eventually master the new thing, and the thing that comes after that. And then after that.

But mastery is never enough. Psychologically, man is forever hungry and the world is a bottomless bag of salted peanuts. We can never get enough. As chronically restless, curious creatures, we need new knowledge; not so much for the satisfaction of having it, but because new knowledge leads to new questions and to still-deeper mysteries. And it is the deeper mysteries we must have to stay alive.

Consider our tools for exploration. If, upon arriving from another solar system, you were going to build the perfect creature to seek out the mysteries of the fishes on planet earth, it seems to me you would design the creature according to the following specifications:

1. The eyes would be mounted high and focus sharply enough to study water as well as a heron and set far enough apart to judge the exact distance to a rising trout. (See osprey for details.)
2. The hands would feature opposing thumbs and be capable of holding anything from a cane pole to deepsea rod.
3. The hands would also be of sufficient delicacy of movement to permit tying #28 midges, big enough to tail an Atlantic salmon and strong enough for horsing in a blue-fin tuna.
4. Bipedal locomotion would be required to get from one pond to the next and from fresh water to salt, and a rolling, mile-eating gait is recommended. Also, the legs would be long enough to permit crossing shallow bodies of water. (See shore birds for examples.)
5. The creature would have a decent nose for water.
6. A brain the size of a large grapefruit would do. It needn't be so heavy as to be burdensome, but it would be big enough to keep track of where it has been and, if possible, where it is going. It would be capable of memorizing the timing of steelhead runs, the tides and the Solunar Tables. Most importantly, there would be no upper limit on what it might dream, imagine or create. It would be able to design and build everything from fishing prams to starships. And it would be built so that it can never be sated.

With such a design, is it any wonder that the first fisherman set off in several directions at once in his search for the treasures of the fishes.

The Treasures of the Fishes

Present everywhere, every one unique, some lovely beyond belief and others a perfect fright, all fishes live below the surface of the water where we can't quite see them. Thus, they are more mysterious to us than the birds or gophers or coyotes. Fishes better tease our curiosity than other creatures. They motivate us to catch them and whet our appetite for mastery.

The mystery of the fishes is a very big one and you need several lifetimes to solve even part of it. Consider that of all the planets known, ours is the only watery one, the only known aquarium in the cosmos. It's a pretty big one at some 300 million cubic miles of water, not counting the tears you carry in your lachrymal glands in case you break off a really big one. Throughout nearly all this water, fishes have been busy evolving into more shapes, sizes, colors, methods of movement, camouflages and special adaptations of defense and offense than you could ever imagine. We have not met them all. Many remain hidden in the depths.

Fishes are by far the most numerous and diverse of creatures who, like us and unlike insects, wear their spinal cords on the inside where they don't show. There are some 32,000 species of fish discovered so far, two-thirds marine and one-third freshwater; compared to only 9,000 species of reptiles and amphibians, 8,900 birds, and a lousy 6,000 mammals. Fishes are the most diverse in size. The difference between the smallest, a quarter-inch-long dwarf pygmy goby, and the largest, the 60-foot, 50-ton whale shark, is much greater than the difference between the smallest mammal, the three-inch Etruscan shrew and the largest, the blue whale.

From the trout you caught last weekend to the blind fishes who live on the floor of the Marianas Trench seven miles below sea level, no other creature has filled nature's wet niches like the fishes.

And some not-so-wet niches. Consider just the catfishes.

There are 15 or more families of catfish, each family containing many species. In diversity catfish are legendary. You've got catfish that talk, catfish that walk and catfish that can't see. Not long ago, research biologists confirmed the existence of a species of small, pink, red-lipped blind catfish living in an aquifer 2,000 feet beneath south-central Texas. Called blind cats, these fishes have been getting along quite nicely over the millions of years they've been trapped in their watery underworld.

There are catfish that can't chew because they're toothless, that wear armor, that live upside down, that are electrified, that can climb out on dry ground and travel crosscountry. There are parasitic catfish, too.

The little least madtom catfish grows to an inch in length while ol' *Siluris glanis* of the Amazon River has been weighed in at 400 pounds. South America has more than most continents, and in North America alone, they go by brown or black bullhead, blues, channel cats, flathead catfish, green bullhead, gaff topsail catfish, headwater catfish, sea catfish, spotted bullhead, stonecat, tadpole madtom, walking catfish, white catfish, yaqui catfish and yellow bullhead.

One of the people who never stopped asking the "why" question was Aristotle, way back in the fourth century B.C. As one of the first scientific students of life on the planet and a fellow with a bad case of curiosity, he took the trouble to record something elemental about catfish. He said, "It deposits its eggs in shallow water, generally close to roots or reeds. The eggs are sticky and adhere to the roots. The female catfish, having laid her eggs, goes away. The male stays on and guards them, keeping off all other little fishes that might steal the eggs or fry . . . In repelling the little fishes, he sometimes makes a rush in the water, emitting a muttering noise by rubbing his gills . . . He thus continues for 40 or 50 days until the young are well grown . . . "

I've caught a lot of catfish over the years. I like catfish. After catching dozens and dozens and dozens from the backwaters of the Boone River near my grandfather's Iowa farm when I was boy, I thought I knew all there ever was to know about catfish. But I didn't know beans.

And I still don't. I could stop what I'm doing right now, turn my remaining years over to the study of catfish, and would be lucky to learn a thousandth of what there is to learn. I'd die with a hundred cat-fishy mysteries still up on the blackboard begging answers. If I decided to go on a catfish-catching odyssey to land one of every kind of catfish, and could get cracking on the project at first light tomorrow, the journey would take me to the end of my string even if I didn't stop to eat any of those wondrous packages of moist, white, flaky protein that, if cooked Cajun style, with plenty of black pepper in a red-hot iron skillet, are simply to die for.

As mysteries for the human mind to puzzle after, fishes never stop. We haven't even caught, let alone know, all the kinds of fishes there probably are. If curiosity is what keeps us going, keeps us vital, keeps us motivated and questing ever onward, ever upward, what better mystery than the fishes? Or how to catch them? Or where to find them? Or how to figure the "whys" of them?

I'm betting that if we go to Mars in the next century, and if its frozen waters ever contained life, or do contain life down deep under the cold surface somewhere, then we will find some kind of fish. And if not on Mars, then at some other stop along the Milky Way.

From what I know of how life gets kick-started from the right mix of hydrogen, oxygen, heat, light and such, if you get it going at all it starts near or under water. If it starts under the waves and needs to travel to survive, it swims. If it swims, it needs gills, fins, a tail, a mouth and a pooper. If it must move quickly and well, it will be torpedo shaped, slick and slimy. If it has gills and fins and a tail and a mouth and a skeleton to hold it all together, and if it looks like a slick torpedo, it seems to me the astronauts better pack a travel rod and some dry flies.

Nope, there will be no end to the mysteries.

So, as I ease out of this writing chair, load the light rods in the truck, and head down to that little canyon where I found the grass pickerel (who knows what swims there that I *didn't* catch), let me leave you with a few pesky "why" and "how-come" questions that have pestered me personally and, in the process, made me grateful to be an angler not only for fish, but for the mysteries of life.

Why are the chain pickerel's chains chained?

Why are bluegill gills blue?

Why do some fish, like bluegills, school?

Why does one species school in the shape of a square, while another species schools in the shape of a diamond?

Why do some schooling fish, when attacked by a predator, close ranks, speed up and assume the shape of one big fish, a fish that looks exactly like them?

And how do they *do* that?

Do schools of fish have a higher IQ than a single fish?

Did fish start out schooling, or have they learned how to school along the evolutionary trail?

Why does a schooling fish like a mackerel, after it's grown big enough to join a school, gradually "forget" how to swim backward?

How do schools of fish sort themselves according to size? Is it because the little guys can't keep up, or because the big guys tell them to back off?

How do the fish on the outside of the school get a job description that says: "Hey! You're the eyes of this outfit, no dozing!"

Can fish sleep while they're schooling along?

How can a whole school of fish change direction within one-sixth of a second?

How did schooling fish come to know and understand the oldest rule of human survival: united we stand, divided we fall?

Are schools of fish coed? If so, does everyone go steady with everyone else, or do they pair off like decent people before having sex?

By what mechanism does a sea-run cutthroat know it's time to start inland to the spawning gravels?

What happens in the brain of smolt when a heron lands nearby?

How do walking catfish know they'll find water?

And will we ever see them in Nikes?

If trout have such small brains, how come they can be so hard to catch?

We know some fishes "talk" (hiss, grunt, chirp, purr, buzz, whistle and bellow), but what are they saying?

If we knew what the crappies were saying, could we figure out how to better catch them?

Do fish recognize each other?

If they do, do the talking ones have greetings?

Finally, if there are catfish living two thousand feet below southwest Texas in an aquifer, how would you catch one, and if you did catch catfish from the Devil's own fishpond, what would they taste like?

The true wonder of the fishes is we will never know them completely. As the naturalist Henry Beston once wrote of the creatures with whom we share the planet and whom, in our arrogance, we wrongly patronize for being lesser forms, "They are not brethren, they are not underlings; they are other nations, caught with ourselves in the net of life and time, fellow prisoners of the splendor and travail of the Earth."

Every fisherman has a grass pickerel to catch, a mystery to solve and a reason to travel hopefully. This book is dedicated to exploring the mysteries while enjoying the journey.

You can't depend on your judgment
when your imagination is out of focus.

— Mark Twain

The Neuropsychology
of Fly Selection

If *why?* is the greatest single question asked by the inquisitive angler, then *what?* is the second greatest question, as in, "What lure should I use?" That we are able to answer this question at all not only gets at what is truly unique about human beings, but also helps explain how fishermen can not only daydream about going fishing, but actually catch fish in those daydreams.

If you define yourself as a fly fisherman, I ask you to close your eyes and imagine a favorite spot on your home waters where you've caught many fish. Other anglers, feel free to apply this to your own methods, spots and species. Now, pick up your rod and make ready to cast. What sort of fly is affixed to your tippet? In an instant, you could tell me. I know this because humans have the mental capacity to call up vivid recordings of past experience and throw them up on the screen we call visual memory.

Even more impressive is this. If I suggest that the fly you're using isn't working, you know exactly what fly to try next. And, if that one fails, the next best fly. The hatch matters, but you can "see" that, too.

Not only can you give me the name of fly and study the water, you can describe the setup in great detail from the picture on your memory's color screen.

How do you do that?

I mean, how do you see yourself fishing in your mind's eye? And what is a "mind's eye" anyway?

How do you remember what lure worked best in this particular spot, and which lure worked next best, third best, and so on?

If you remember all this stuff, where do you store it?

How do you store it?

If you have all these lures and flies and fishing spots filed away somewhere, how do you completely forget some of them over time and yet remember them when you return for a visit, and remember all of them under hypnosis?

How do you do something as weird and wonderful as select the perfect fly for exact fishing conditions you only imagine? How do you do something no other type of fisher can do?

Ospreys can't do it. Cormorants can't do it. Sea otters don't carry around a favorite rock for busting clam shells like a bass fisherman carries around a favorite minnow plug. No, only human fishers can imagine going fishing, imagine where to fish, imagine what to fish with, imagine what they'll catch, and imagine how much to stretch the truth about the one they imagine might get away.

"Imagination," as Anatole France said, "is everything."

The primary activity of the human mind is imagination. When we dream of fishing, this is our only reality. When not on the water or otherwise occupied, fishermen live in dream time, in images. Without an image, a dream, a desire or hope, there is no life worth living.

Just exactly how and why and through what mental processes an angler studies the lures lying in his tackle box or the flies stuck to his hat band, and then decides which one will probably work best, is one of the greatest mysteries of human consciousness. And while I love a mystery as much as the next fellow, I try not to think too much about this particular one for fear that someday, when the trout are being too selective and I can't imagine the proper fly to fool them with, I'll end up with a broken decision-maker like the poor centipede in the poem:

> *The centipede was quite happy*
> *Until the toad in fun*
> *Said, "Pray which leg comes after which?"*
>
> *Which brought it to such a pitch*
> *It lay distracted in a ditch*
> *Considering how to run.*

Neuropsychology 101

For ten years in the middle of my career as a clinical psychologist, I specialized in what was then the new and developing field of neuropsychology, basically a field of highly specialized study and practice having to do with the relationship between brain function and behavior. The neuropsychologist's job, among other things, is to examine a patient's behavior, symptoms, responses to standardized and elaborate test questions, reaction time to various tasks, motor coordination, sensory capacities, expressive abilities, concentration, attention, memory functions, intellect, judgment, reasoning powers and all sorts of other things that, when all the data are collected and analyzed, tell us if there is anything wrong with the old bean.

Neuropsychologists do this better than just about anyone, and for the years I worked patients up for other specialists, I had a high old time puzzling out what was right and wrong with people's noodles — tumors, frontal lobe insults, stroke damage, alcohol dementia and so on.

Neuropsychology grew more and more technical, there were more and more "essential" journals to read, more workshops to attend, and one day I found myself marginally qualified. Rather than try to catch up and keep up with a specialty that kept pulling away and getting ahead of the general practitioner, I quit the field and withdrew to other pleasures. However, I still remember enough to explain some of the "how" of the angler's brain, and at least some of the mysteries of lure selection — including why Willy, the World's Greatest Fisherman, catches more fish than you and I.

The World's Greatest Fisherman

I've created a character called Willy Wonder, the World's Greatest Fisherman. He's cut out of some whole cloth left over from an old fishing shirt. I created Willy for two reasons: first, without a guy like Willy and a little humor, neuropsychology will bore you stiffer than a shark rod, and second, every fisherman alive hopes to become a better fisherman.

First and most importantly, if you want to become a great fisherman like Willy Wonder, buckle your seat belt. I say this with all the gravity of someone who has examined many patients who used their heads to dent dashboards, bend steering wheels and shatter windshields, thus damaging the most sensitive, delicate, wonderful fishcatching instrument ever evolved from star dust: the human brain. This three-pound knob of neurons, fibers and gentle chemical reactions at the end of your spinal cord is the best single piece of fishing tackle you will ever own. So don't slam it around in crashing cars. Willy doesn't. End of obligatory neuropsychological health warning and sermonette.

The brain and nervous system are organized, in the simplest terms, as an electrochemical communication system enabling us to think, feel, wade streams and cast flies with a single backcast. Deep in the middle, in the so-called primitive brain, are vital functions like breathing and the pleasure centers. The uppermost, outermost part of the brain is divided into two halves. Distinctive parts include an occipital lobe in the rear for vision, temporal lobes lower down on each side like saddlebags for speech and hearing, parietal lobes higher up on each side for sensory and motor input and execution, and the frontal lobes for fishing.

Well, sort of.

You need pretty much your entire brain to become a Willy Wonder, especially the cerebral cortex. That's an eighth-inch-thick sheet of billions of nerve cells with around 100 trillion interconnective contacts that, even if you have a Ph.D. in neurobiology, is considerably more difficult to unravel than the worst monofilament tangle you've ever had. All the truly interesting questions left about human behavior lie inside this thin, layered neural bird's nest for which, because live fishermen are slow to volunteer their brains for research projects, gaining new information is both slow and tedious.

Now, when you consider that all these cells are, somehow, connected to one another through a maze of electrochemical and ever-changing physical processes, the human brain quickly becomes the most complex structure in the known universe. The product of millions of years of evolution (or a touch of God's finger), the human brain is our only means of survival now and into the coming centuries. It allows fishermen to do everything from match the hatch of a small black caddis to remember "a time when . . ."

It is well established now that the interval between the hit and hooking of a fish is represented in the individual nerve cell by the convergence of two different chemical signals (calcium and serotonin) on the same neural enzyme. The 0.5-second interval may correspond to the time during which calcium is elevated in the presynaptic terminal and binds to calmodulin so as to prime the adenylyl cyclase to produce more cyclic AMP in response to the serotonin.

If you understood that last sentence then you no doubt already have a Ph.D. in one of the neurosciences and obviously don't spend enough time fishing. For the rest of us, all we need to know is that, when it comes to being better fishermen, all our learning flows in the forward direction, following the arrow of time. What's most interesting is that, as one neuron shakes hands chemically with another, the brain actually changes. And I mean in an architectural sense.

The beams and posts and nails and mortar and baling wire that hold all those billions of cells together inside our heads actually rearrange themselves and grow. Like some fantastic high school lab experiment, the brain, as it learns, becomes something different, something new, something that has never existed in the universe before. Even as you read this paragraph your brain is changing itself to accommodate these ideas. It's a simple leap, then, to the axiom that the superior fisherman is always the result of intelligent effort. Learning effort. Which is why I invented Willy Wonder.

To answer the questions of which fly to use, where to cast it, and how to get to a far river on time for a particular hatch, you simply must have a decent set of frontal lobes. With an intact cortex and a good set of frontals, you can plan fishing trips into next week, next month, next year and even into whatever afterlife suits you. You can even keep track of which fishing lies you told to whom. Which is why I warned you about seat belts. While there are no good brain injuries, sustaining a frontal lobe injury is sort of like breaking off the last two feet of your favorite fly rod; you can still fish with it, but most of the thrill is gone.

Willy Wonder has a perfect set of frontal lobes. He's taken good care of them. In fact, Willy wears cleats on his waders so he won't fall on slippery rocks, bang his brain on a boulder, and forget how to tie a Royal Coachman. Result: Willy's frontals take good care of him.

So, without getting too technical here, how does Willy select the right fly to catch so damn many fish?

How Willy Wonder Catches Fish

The first thing Willy does is get rid of randomness in his fishing. One-celled bacteria like E. coli wander randomly, tumbling and swimming through their watery environments until they come upon a food source. Then, with their little bitty "brains," sensing devices, really, they stop tumbling long enough to eat up what is close by. When the food is gone, they start tumbling again until they eventually stumble onto another source of nourishment. They may get lucky and multiply and carry on as bacteria have been carrying on since the beginning.

There is nothing wrong with random search; it's just not a very efficient way to find fish quickly. I've seen fishermen fish a new lake with the E. coli random search method, and while they do catch fish, you won't see Willy fishing with them. It is one thing to conduct a random search for fish in a trout stream and quite another to start a random search in Lake Erie. Random search, trial-and-error and by-guess-and-by-golly are, however, the means and processes by which the human brain evolved into the highly efficient fishing instrument it is today.

We know how randomness followed by selection worked when the first fisherman made the first fishing knife. Although we don't have a video, we can tell by the piles of broken rocks he left behind that, while bashing together two potato-sized granite stones, he made a large pile of random-sized and-shaped chips, and then *selected* the sharpest one — probably with a right-hand grip. The more bashed rocks, the more possibilities a really good "knife" might appear. The chip that would best slice open the belly of a big perch or whack off the head of a rainbow got selected as a cutting tool.

Next time you're out on a stream, if the law permits, try making your own filleting knife — it works, but watch your fingers.

Selecting from Randomness

Basically, the more random casts you make, the greater the chance you will eventually catch a fish — which is one reason every fisher-man I know has trouble quitting and wants to make "one last cast." Succeed on that cast, and that is the first cast you will "select" on your next trip back.

If you like to tie original trout flies and eventually stumble on one that works better than all others, you will probably select this pattern for future use, share it with pals, and hopefully introduce it to the rest of the fly fishing fraternity, thus becoming famous but not rich.

The rule of untutored human learning is to bash rocks together, keep putting out random casts and stray ideas until, when something finally works, looks right, feels right or sounds right, it gets selected, "clicks" into the neural pathways, and is stored in those old neuro-chemical memory banks so that it can be passed along to younger fishermen. Thus, down through our long history of random new ideas, we humans have selected, saved and improved upon every good idea from fishhooks to symphonies.

Despite its inefficiencies, I enjoy a random search for new waters and new fishes, but I generally pack a lunch and don't have to have a fish dinner to survive.

All organisms must solve problems to survive. All living things are more or less in constant search of a better deal and a higher standard of living. From the lowly bacteria tumbling through pond water in search of duck droppings to the guy in the fly shop buying a new Orvis five-weight pack rod, we all have to gamble a little to find a better deal than the one we've got.

Eliminating Randomness

There are several ways Willy Wonder avoids the inefficiency of ran-dom casts with random lures. Because experience amounts to the elim-ination of bad guesses, Willy has already laid aside what lures probably won't work. Thanks to a highly developed functional memory, he al-ready knows it's tough to get a big bass to rise to a No. 14 Adams. Willy also remembers how few trout he's caught on a Hula Popper. So when he goes to the bass pond he leaves his trout flies at home. Willy and every other fisherman who ever went fishing a first time should be just a little smarter than he was awhile ago or, as I like to think of it, he should have reduced a little randomness in his tumbling.

Because of the brain's ability to store vast amounts of information based on firsthand experience, even young, inexperienced fishermen can become old, know-it-all fishermen very quickly. It is quite possi-ble, given the human brain's amazing capacity for learning, to become a spiny ray fishing instructor after catching your very first bluegill.

The second reason Willy repeatedly wins First-Biggest-Most fish-ing contests is that he uses *other fishermen's* memories. In strange country, he hires guides and does not stand on pride. He is able to access great quantities of information stored in the brains of other anglers who, through their own experiences, have changed the very nature of the way their brains are organized.

Contrary to the rumor that you can't find one big enough to study, research shows that fisher brains actually undergo physical and neuro-chemical changes as they acquire new information. We're talking about growing new neural tissue, increasing the complexity and rich-ness of connections between neurons, and structural changes in the fundamental operations of the brain itself. This process is called synap-togenesis.

Some humans, and especially adolescents, consider it beneath them-selves to learn from others, but Willy doesn't. He knows that other fisher-men have eliminated lots and lots of bad guesses through their own random tumbling and selection efforts. And to the degree to which other anglers are willing to share their mistakes and successes, Willy is able to absorb this knowledge, store it in his own neurochemical memory banks and thus stand on the shoulders of others to spot fish to cast to. These sources of information include fishing writers, lec-turers, professional guides, the guy in the next boat and garrulous old grandfathers. Fishermen willing to take a hand up from other fisher-men are using their neural networks to maximum advantage.

The third reason Willy catches more fish than just about anybody but a cormorant is that he is better able than most to imagine the fu-ture and what sort of lure might work. This is the tricky part of the neuropsychology of fly selection, but it also the most interesting.

Scenario Spinning

It is our ability to close our eyes and spin visual scenarios into some uncertain future that so fascinates students of human psychology. That we can line up, sort through, order from top to bottom and fully anticipate the consequences of one decision over any number of other decisions is, when you stop to think about it and even when you don't, an absolutely amazing feat. It's as if you can live your life before it happens, decide what you like and what you don't like, and proceed directly to the good times.

Unfortunately, not everyone does this, or is able to do it. Seriously brain-injured folks can't, but even more tragic is that lots and lots of normal people with normal brains never bother to imagine how things might be, but rather tuck their head under their arm, look straight down at the way things are and follow the ruts in the road. While I have no proof, I think fishermen who take this approach to life also forget to keep their hooks sharp. Fishing and learning to fish should open the mind, not close it.

It is this ability to imagine what fly might work best on some future river at some future date that makes us humans so much fancier than lizards and lions. Willy, with his magnificent, and some say "accidental," human brain, is able to see tomorrow in his head, turn it around and over and upside down, judge the weather before it appears and then pretend enough possible situations and lures and fishing conditions to not only pack his gear accordingly, but to compute the future into probability statements, including the probable time and place of the next Clark Fork River stonefly hatch.

They're Probably Biting

A probability statement is nothing more than a statement of odds, a way to put numbers on possible outcomes. For example, the odds are that if you use a Light Cahill instead of a black ant pattern during a sulfur mayfly hatch, you will catch more brown trout. Fifty percent more? Seventy-five percent? The exact number doesn't matter. What matters is that the human brain is so organized that probability theory and odds-making are quite reasonable exercises, thus making our predictions act and sound like real science. Other things being equal, and outrageous luck notwithstanding, the angler who makes the best predictions catches the most fish. The best fishermen are the best odds makers. In the long run, luck has little to do with fishing success.

It is our ability to foretell the probable consequences of casting a particular lure into a particular water, *without having to actually cast it*, that allows fishermen to justify not one, but several tackle boxes; one for big lake trout, one for walleyes, one for bass and crappies, one for saltwater, etc. Fly fishermen, so loaded down with frontal lobes they have trouble balancing while they wade, are such a highly specialized form of fisherman that their randomness-reducing, anticipatory tackle requirements stagger the imagination. In fact, I know fly fishermen who own enough gear to equip several small towns.

The last thing Willy does better than most of us is to use his neurons to plan, perfect and polish his fishing skills. To plan a successful fishing trip he uses spare memory banks called checklists so as not to forget the rods, the waders, the gas or the toilet paper. I can think of nothing that better reflects the good uses to which that bundle of neurons at the top of your neck can be put than a perfect fishing plan. A good plan is a thing of beauty and a dream with wheels. And no matter how good the plan, it can always be improved upon, year after year.

To perfect and polish the motor skills of knot-tying, casting, wading and landing fish, Willy is in constant training. He keeps his motor skills tuned, his timing on and his habits oiled. He is, basically, a superior predator never out of practice. If you worry about all the time you spend daydreaming about hooking and landing some wily fish, sports psychology research confirms that imagining your lightning-fast hook set again and again and again helps you set the hook faster *in real time* out on the water. Daydreaming, then, is mental practice, rehearsing motor skills in your mind and a dress rehearsal for the real thing. It should be encouraged.

Consider the neuropsychology of knot tying.

When first learning a motor skill like tying the Bimini Twist, a great deal of attention and concentration is required. You must not only "see" how to tie a Bimini, but you must actually use your eyes and hands and fingers to tie the darned thing.

However, when the knot is tied again and again and again, the brain changes and "grows" until less neural energy is required for the job. Once the eyes, fingers and brain all get going in the same direction and new neural connections for the Bimini are established topside, the brain seems to say to the spinal cord, "Look, buddy, this Bimini Twist is getting bo-o-oring. You tie it from now on." Soon the fisherman is unconsciously tying Bimini Twists at the spinal level and simultaneously inventing fishing lies with his cerebral cortex.

Once we humans master motor skills like tying fishing knots or riding a bicycle down deep in the brain and spinal cord, we essentially never forget them. You can learn to ride a bike when you're nine, stop riding at 19, and get back on one when you're 90 and, after just a wobble or two, off you go down the street pedaling as if you never missed a beat. Same with tying a Bimini Twist or a trout fly or double hauling fly line or spin casting a bass plug "tight to the pads."

Choices

If there is such a thing as free will, my guess is that it's our ability to imagine the stream we're headed to and then, ever so carefully, to play out the possible flies we might use to get that first trout to fall for the imitation. We visualize the pool we want to hit first, see its smooth surface, consider the many choices and probabilities encased in our fly box, and then, remembering it is August and grasshopper season, quickly flip through an index of patterns, recall how well a yellow-bodied Joe's Hopper worked last time out, and bingo, we've exercised that divine ability to choose.

Humans have been beating around the idea of choice and free will for a long time. Considering the ideals of democracy and the rights of man, it seems we all want, cherish and are even willing to die for what I like to call a deliberate future.

A deliberate future is much different than a random future; in a deliberate future you can dream up a possibility, plan for it and then, so long as it doesn't hurt anyone else and you live in a free country, carry out that future just as you dreamed it. It is your personal, one-of-a-kind future and nobody can or should be able take it away from you. To me, this is what being human is all about; spinning out possibilities and living the ones you like. It is why ideas like freedom, liberty and self-determination have so much currency in the hearts of people and particularly in the hearts of fishermen.

Now, since this is March and the first hatch of sulfur duns is due off Rock Lake by mid-May, I think I'll go down to the fly-tying bench and whip out a dozen Light Cahills. Without even closing my eyes, I can see those big browns rising here now to slurp down emergers before their wings are quite dry enough to lift them off. My arm almost twitches as I set an imaginary hook and feel an imaginary surge of power shoot up my imaginary rod.

After a lifetime of fishing, it's nice to have the majority of my random tumbling behind me.

*I still don't know why I fish or why
other men fish, except that we like it
and it makes us think and feel.*

— **Roderick Haig-Brown,**
A River Never Sleeps

Pavlov's Trout

For the intelligent readership of this book, Dr. Ivan Pavlov's name should ring a bell. For others, it may only cause them to salivate slightly. The good doctor is best remembered for his work on classical conditioning; the pairing of an unknown stimulus with a known one to alter behavior. While I doubt Pavlov made the connection himself, this winner of the 1904 Nobel Prize in physiology and world-famous psychologist may have stumbled upon the very essence of sport fishing and why we all love it so.

I think this footnote to the history of psychology will give fishermen everywhere something to add to those late-night, campfire conversations when some know-it-all is begging to have his leader shortened.

The Case of the Difficult Dog

Those who recall Pavlov's original work in classical conditioning remember that his experiments involved placing a hungry dog in a harness on a metal table and ringing a bell at the same time he presented a meat powder for dinner. Dogs naturally salivate to meat powder. Ringing bells only annoy them. However, once there were sufficient pairings of ringing bells and meat powder, the sound of the bell alone caused the dog to salivate.

The dependent variables Pavlov measured to see how his experiments were going were occurrence of saliva and how much saliva the dog emitted as the number of bell and meat powder pairings increased. Dr. Pavlov eventually proved what every camp cook who ever rang a dinner bell knows. Hungry critters come running *and* drooling.

Actually, this research is much more complicated than I've described, but the fundamental idea is that one of the ways creatures learn is through associations of one thing with another, provided, of course, the creature will stand still for the training.

Enter the difficult dog.

Of the hundreds of dogs Pavlov used in his experiments, most were cooperative. They allowed the researchers to pet them, feed them, care for them and, when the time came, they would jump up on the metal table, allow themselves to be strapped in, and the experiments would begin.

Not our hero.

A mixed breed not described in the original research reports, this dog was friendly and appeared no different from the others. However, as soon as it was placed on the table and restrained, it would begin to struggle. It whined, barked, scratched, strained and chewed at its leather harnesses. It salivated when it wasn't supposed to. No matter how much Pavlov and his colleagues reassured and calmed the poor beast, it kept up a constant protest until the experimenters wearied of the whole affair, removed the straps and placed the dog back in its cage.

After resting the dog for periods of a few days up to as much as three months on one occasion, it was returned to the lab for study. Restricted again by the harness, the dog instantly launched yet another struggle to break free.

Each time a training session began, the dog protested, and each time the protests got worse, never better. Pavlov remarked that maybe this subject had a wild ancestor somewhere in its pedigree. Otherwise, why wouldn't it accept captivity? Pavlov also noted he had seen fully wild, caged animals eventually give up their struggle to be free, refuse food, sicken and die. We can trust this never happened to our hero. Pavlov was kind to his dogs.

Pavlov never did condition the difficult dog to salivate to the sound of a ringing bell. Defeated by the mutt, he salvaged his efforts with what, in those early days of reflexology, he called, "The Reflex of Freedom." He knew, like researchers everywhere, that it was far better to come up with a new, never-before-described phenomenon than admit failure and endanger his funding source.

The Freedom Reflex, as described by Pavlov trying to make sense of the difficult dog, is inborn as opposed to learned, present in all creatures, basic and unchanging. It is a self-preserving reflex and, if not expressed with vigor, places the individual and his kind at risk of death and extinction. To quote Dr. Pavlov, "All animals deprived of their usual freedom strive to liberate themselves, especially wild animals captured for the first time." This was a brave statement from a man working and writing in Communist Russia in the 1920s and '30s.

The Freedom Reflex in Fishes

A lot of fishermen these days say things like, "Oh, I don't care if I catch fish, just so long as I can be out there in nature." Or, "I just like the scenery, you know, the trees, the sky . . ." Or, "I love the sound of water lapping against the side of the boat. Catching fish is a bonus."

These remarks sound sportsmanlike and ecologically responsible and so forth, but you and I know that people go fishing to catch fish.

If you really don't care if you catch fish when you go fishing, can you be a true fisherman? I don't think so. I have yet to meet a fisherman who could look me square in the eye and say without flinching, "It's true, I *really* don't care if I catch fish." You don't have to keep them, eat them, photograph or frame them, but you do have to catch them, at least once in a while.

So, I have asked myself, "Just what is it we true fishermen are after anyway?"

Dr. Pavlov may have the answer in his Freedom Reflex and later observations on the nature of wild things. His findings can be briefly summed up as follows:

1. When trapped or suddenly restricted from natural movement, *all* creatures immediately do two things: struggle to break free and, if able, reorient themselves.
2. Once free and reoriented, the creature will, in the next split second, make good its escape.

This behavior is fundamental to survival, so the creature can be counted upon to put every ounce of energy into it.

Except for a totally exhausted, near-dead fish, any angler who has freed his quarry after a hard fight has observed what Dr. Pavlov observed. Suddenly released from hook and hand, the fish rests momentarily in the water, righting itself and checking its bearings, and then, *swoosh*, it's gone!

Fish who don't fight to break free, reorient and escape in the underwater world also go by another name: supper. Predatory search and capture of one fish by another has been going on beneath the waves for 400 million years or more, so this set of reflexes has been strongly selected and is by now hard-wired into the neural circuitry of all fishes. Only by breaking free and making a dash to safety do they stand a chance of growing up to spawn fry of their own.

Whether Pavlov's Freedom Reflex exists in nonwild, hatchery-raised fish remains undetermined, but we know from studies on zoo-raised animals that, once returned to their wild environments, they often become confused, helpless and unable to elude their natural predators; the very predators, by the way, that helped them evolve into successful wild animals in the first place. Many wild-trout advocates disdain hatchery fish precisely because they are too stupid to protect themselves and stupid fish do not make good sport.

Could this be nature's equation?

No Freedom Reflex equals no freedom equals no species!

The Thrill of Predation

If you sort through all the things fishing includes — daydreaming, rod-building, fly-tying, camping, scenery, solitude, friendship, the love of nature, tradition, relaxation, a balm for the soul and so on — what you find at the very core of angling is the thrill of getting hold of a wild thing, a creature who will, reliably and predictably, spend its entire essence in a struggle to break free from bondage.

This is the thrill of the hook-up, the catch.

Fish don't fight half-assed battles; they go to the mat every time. To us it may be sport, but to the fish it is life or death. Studies on fish locomotion and physiology tell us that only during so-called "burst" swimming, in a feeding chase or while engaged in Pavlov's Freedom Reflex, do fishes switch to anaerobic metabolism and kick in all the muscle groups so as to maximize velocity, endurance and, God bless 'em, sharp turns.

While it is good to feel the nibble or the take or see the strike, and it is wonderful to set the hook, these serve only to trigger our autonomic nervous systems into the same state of high arousal as our prey's. What really keeps our predator's heart pumping is the all-out struggle of the just-hooked fish to break free. The harder it fights, the greater the rush, the greater the thrill.

While I'm not sure fish have spirits, it is clear that if they do, a two-pound smallmouth has a huge fighting spirit, whereas a two-pound walleye has to swagger considerably not to be called a coward. In the relationship between fishermen and fish, we measure a fish's spirit by how well, once hooked, it struggles to free itself. I like catching carp because, once hooked, a carp never quits. A hooked carp seems to say, "Okay, buddy. Now that you fooled me, let's go ahead and see if you can pull me out, or if I can pull you in. Loser dies."

The quality of a fish's struggle is why I like bluegill over crappies, rainbows over cutthroats, most saltwater fish over fresh, and catfish all the time because they'll horn you anytime, anywhere, in water or out. A really good fight is, when it's all said and done, what I most want.

I'm sure an ichthyologist would correct me about what it is that goes into a given fish's ability to fight — bone structure, musculature, fin height and width and such — but, in the same way that I don't want an astronomer to remind me that the constellation Pisces is a projection of man's imagination onto a random grouping of distant galaxies, I like to keep my illusions about the fishes intact. When I'm out socializing with them, I want to meet fish who remind me of what is admirable about both them and us: a willingness to fight hard to stay free, and the harder the better.

Of one thing I am deeply convinced: if the fishes don't need us, we most certainly need them. If a fish runs and jumps and shakes its head or dives into the weeds or wraps my line around a submerged log, or just bows its neck and bulls it out with me, then at least I know I've met a creature who wants its freedom as much as I want mine. Maybe that's why fishing should be a sacred act, an interaction with another creature that should never be taken lightly.

The Wildness Factor

In mulling over Pavlov's observations about the Freedom Reflex, I have wondered if it is the wildness in fish that somehow renews the wildness in us. After the hook is set and the shiver of something wild comes dancing up the rod, we seem somehow to be released from the confines of our overcivilized selves. It is as if the fighting fish is the longed-for iron key that opens the golden door to our uncensored souls and what might be still wild in us.

I have seen children squeal, women scream and men bellow with delight at the first mad run of a just-hooked fish. I have heard their voices and my own ring out over a still lake. And in that instant, in that moment of abandonment to pure, uncluttered joy, there is, suddenly and momentarily, a brief glimpse into the untamed, unfettered, wild nature of what man once was, and what he still needs to be from time to time.

And afterward, after the fish is brought to hand, the catcher seems

somehow recharged, revitalized, renewed. Having shed the burden of self-consciousness, if only for a few moments, he seems somehow relaxed and more at one with his nature.

Sometimes after a good fight with a strong fish, and after I have set us both free, I simply reel in and head home knowing, deep down, that no finer moment will fill up my soul as well that day. And it's a good going-home feeling indeed.

If there is any merit to my thesis that wildness can be transmitted from one species to another over something so tenuous as a fishing line, then it seems our connections to what little wildness and wilderness is left in our world should be even more precious to us than any of us have yet realized.

To mirror the fishes we angle for one last time, it seems to me that we all need wildness — deep in our souls, but also at our fingertips. We need ready access to it. We need to be able to touch this wildness, to call it forth when we need it, up and out of the padded cell in which we keep it locked for civilization's sake.

On those days when we feel gang hooked ourselves, and are headed inexorably toward the gaff or landing net, we need to call upon our wildness to struggle to break away, to right ourselves, and to make good our dash to freedom.

Thank you, Dr. Pavlov.

Fish, to taste right, must swim three times
— in water, in butter and in wine.

— Polish Proverb

Of Curious Connections

If Dr. Pavlov's observation that creatures are possessed of an urgency to free themselves from captivity, and if my notions about the transmission of wildness from wild fish to the fisher be true, then our other connections with the fishes should be long, deep, broad and complex.

Let us see whither these interconnecting paths may lead.

The Wading Boy

Of all the physical, mental, spiritual and emotional connections we make with the fishes, the one we make with rod, line and lure puts us in closest contact with the fish's wildness. A boy wading a creek with a willow pole, a length of line and a hook rigged with a grasshopper is physically and sensually much closer to his quarry than a man watching his sonar with his downrigger rod in a holder as he trolls over 90 feet of water.

The wading boy is *in* the world of fishes, while the trolling man remains above it, aloof, distant and separated. The boy has closed with nature and experiences fishing through all his senses: touch, smell, sound, taste and vision. Even if our boy catches but a single small trout, such close personal contact with the world of fishes enhances the experience fishermen so hunger for.

The man in the big water boat risks losing his connection to nature and the nature of fishes. Not only is he physically remote — he doesn't even hold his own rod — but his reliance on technology reduces his relationship with the fishes to one with robotics.

I have been both the boy and the man, and I'm fairly certain they have yet to make the gadget to replace the joys of grass stains and grasshoppers. The wonderment of seeing a single little trout rise from its lie to swat a 'hopper and hooking that trout and reeling it in to hold it wet and wriggly in your hand is psychologically much different than watching a monitor for electronic blips, seeing the rigger rod release and netting a huge lake trout. Catching the little trout is like gently running your fingers along the brush strokes of a fine oil painting. Hooking and gaffing a sonar image is like roller-skating through the Louvre. Both fishermen can say they connected with a trout, but there ends any psychological, emotional or spiritual similarity.

The Aquarium Factor

I once kept an aquarium in my consulting office, and not just a freshwater aquarium, but a saltwater layout complete with pumps to recreate the surf and tidal movements of the reef from which my captives came. I had heaters, filters, genuine ocean salt to mix with fresh water, and every sort of tropical fish and shrimp and sea urchin that could live together without killing each other off at, as I quickly learned, rather steep replacement costs. I kept my little set piece of sea life on a stand just opposite my patient's chair.

I might still have the aquarium except for two things: I learned many of the fishes were being illegally and dangerously taken with cyanide, threatening some species and the reefs on which they lived by overfishing; and, while away for a weekend, the power went out. The carnage wreaked in my salt tank by the sudden drop in temperature was unacceptable. I pulled the plug for good.

I never went fishing in my aquarium, though after learning about the 400-year-old art of tanago fishing in Japan and receiving a complete hook, line and sinker outfit much smaller than a dime from a friend's father, I gave it serious thought.

Tanago are tiny, wild fish that live in the rivers and streams of Central Japan. As they approach lunker dimensions, they may run up to an inch long. Fishing with three-foot wands of split bamboo and a beetle larva or quail-egg-batter bait, wading Japanese anglers hold major tanago competitions each year to determine who can catch the most fish in a limited period of time. I understand they are very tasty pan-fried with a little soy sauce. I don't know if you fillet them first or just eat 'em, guts, head and all.

But I digress.

Some people do fish in their aquariums — or their swimming pools, as a pal of mine did after he stocked his with largemouth bass. People build thousands of ponds every year in which to keep fish, sometimes for fishing and sometimes just to feed and care for finny things and to enhance wildlife habitat. At the moment, there is a modest push on by the federal government to help citizens build wildlife ponds, reflood their wetlands, and return water to the surface of the planet where it was once more naturally dispersed and where it seems to do the most good.

Catching fish in one place and moving them to another to keep them alive for the visual pleasure they provide has been going on for at least 4,000 years. Sumerians kept fish in decorative pools apparently designed for viewing pleasure. The Romans kept fish and eels as pets, but it wasn't until the advent of the glass aquarium only a century or so ago that fishermen, fish lovers, naturalists and scientists really got rolling on this business of fish keeping, now a multi-million dollar industry.

I think what happens between the aquarist and his wards is something akin to the pleasure reported by the voyeur. You get to see what goes on in the private lives of fish without them knowing you're watching. Except for the opportunities brought by the recent advent of the Aqua-Lung, we air breathers have traditionally been denied a look beneath the waves. Whatever lies under that glinting surface is fundamentally alien to us. We don't belong there, and we shouldn't go peeking where we don't belong.

This, of course, makes us mad to do it.

A Little More Pepper, Please

Catch-and-release fishing is new and catch-and-release into captivity only a bit older, but catch-and-eat fishing goes all the way back to the original rule of the sea: If it fits in your mouth, it's yours. If it tastes good and doesn't kill you, put it on the menu.

Man's gustatorial connection to the fishes is historically obscure. No one knows when we started eating fish, but our modern-day palate is primed and ready. Of the meats available, fish is now at the head of the health food list and, according to Anne Fletcher in her recent book, *Eat Fish, Live Better*, eating fish is not only healthy as hell, but trendy to boot. I am always gladdened to find something I have been doing for years and years and *years* is suddenly both healthy and trendy. It makes me feel smart as a whip.

Which reminds me of the relationship of eating fish to smartness. Fish has always been considered "brain food." I eat almost as much fish as an osprey, so surely there must be some truth to this. Of course, I'm only joking, and actually, when I was boy I didn't much care for fish and on Fridays was always glad my family wasn't Catholic.

Our attitudes toward everything from who is proper company, or racism, to what is fit to eat, or foodism, are shaped long before our sixth birthday. Most American fishermen never examine why they don't eat carp. I've even heard gefilte fish referred to as "boiled carp wrapped in mucus." This is foodism of the worst kind.

Practically everyone on the planet except non-Jewish, non-Scandinavian middle-class Americans connects to carp with their taste buds. It is one of the main dishes served by the Chinese to visiting dignitaries. The irony is our European grandparents brought carp to this country as a food fish. Outside of a few annoying bones and some unpalatable dark meat that can be easily cut away, carp has a rich, distinctive flavor.

The social psychology of attitude development and how fixed our prejudices can become is the study of how humans learn from one another. Our gustatorial connections to the fishes are heavily influenced by what we learn at home.

The attitudes toward fish we inherit at home can be summed up in the anecdote about the two traveling salesmen in a New York deli:

> *Louisiana Man:* Give me the catfish fillet with a side of chips.
> *Utah Man:* Catfish! Yuuuk! Do you know where catfish live?
>   On the bottom of muddy rivers and ponds. They eat dead
>   stuff. When you think of where that catfish has been, how
>   can you put it in your mouth?
> *Waitress to Utah Man:* So, sir, what'll you have?
> *Utah Man:* I'll take the egg salad sandwich.

Unless attitudes have changed, you still won't find catfish on many restaurant menus in Logan, Utah, and you cannot *not* find hush puppies, those small balls of deep-fried cornbread served with catfish, on any menus in Baton Rouge.

Luckily, our attitudes about what fish we consider fit to eat can be changed. *Sunset* magazine, an authority on what is fit cuisine for the American family, ran a story some years back on the merits of various catfish recipes. Now the whole country eats catfish and catfish farming is very big business.

The new fish and health story is pretty simple. People who live in Greenland or Japan and others who eat a lot of fish don't suffer much cardiovascular disease, the number-one killer in America. If you're a fisherman with a personal or family history of heart disease, the very best thing you can do for yourself is to eat a lot of fish; which means, of course, you have to go fishing more. This is a big responsibility to yourself and those counting on you to survive to a ripe old age, but who's going to do it if you don't?

The magic bullet against heart disease and vascular problems that can affect brain function is fish oils rich in a fatty acid called "omega-3." I don't know enough chemistry to bore you with the makeup and action of this little fatty acid, but remember that all fresh fish contain some.

According to the *New England Journal of Medicine*, fish flesh is also good for the following:

Your circulatory system. The better your blood gets around your body, top to bottom, the warmer your feet will stay when you're winter steelheading or ice fishing.

Your immune system. With a tough immune system, able to fight off whatever bug is going around, you won't get sick and will have even more time to go fishing.

As a cancer fighter. At least some evidence points to eating fish as a way to reduce the risk of various forms of cancer, which also translates into more fishing time.

Migraines. Some early research suggests people who eat fish or take fish oil pills may experience relief from migraine headaches. I've never had a migraine, but I understand they are much less fun even than losing a nice bass.

If fishermen ever needed an excuse to catch-and-eat those fishes of which we have plenty, like crappies, bluegills and sea perch, the American Heart Association and the National Academy of Sciences are standing right behind them, ready to prescribe the low-fat, naturally light nature of fish as one of the very best health foods around.

Apparently, this message has gotten through. There are fish dishes on the menus of fancy restaurants where there were none a few years ago. My friends at DJ's Restaurant & Lounge just over the hill from my home on the shores of, and I'm not making this up, Fish Lake, offer the usual salmon and cod and such, and also *three* kinds of catfish: deep-fried, black-pan, and Cajun style. When I'm not fly-fishing brookies in front of the restaurant, I'm dining on brain food inside the restaurant.

It seems to me that Americans, including the American fishing fra-
ternity-sorority, have pretty narrow prejudices about what is fit to eat
that comes from the deep, and this is too bad. I got over my prejudices against wet-and-slimy food sources early in life thanks, primar-
ily, to a few bad cooks in the U.S. Army.

As a defense against anorexia and the risk of poisoning, I spent a
lot of time off-base foraging for grub in the countryside. The countryside was Japan, and if you live off the land in Japan, you're really living off the sea.

If you take a gracious and experimental gustatorial attitude toward
the sea and all of its edible possibilities, the Japanese will quickly
convert you to everything from smoked squid to pickled octopus. This
exposure of the palate to the law of the sea allowed me to binge on
sushi in Chicago, gorge on fresh-caught, deep-fried sardines along the
Spanish coast, stuff myself with broiled dorado I caught on a fly from
the Sea of Cortez, slurp bouillabaisse made from the rich offering of
British Columbia's Barklay Sound, and enjoy deep-fried piranha in the
Amazon rain forest. When asked how I can eat the same bright or-
ange flesh of the very same mussels I once used for fish bait, I tell folks
that, like all human beings, I'm an omnivore — an omnivore that
fishes.

Because the buyer cannot control the history of store-bought fish,
the sport fisherman has a great advantage in getting in on the best
eating. Dehydration, bacterial growth, high-temperatures and enzyme
activity have such a powerful effect on fish flesh that the great fish
markets of Tokyo age fish by the minute and price accordingly. At an
expensive Japanese sushi house positioned over an inlet to the Sea of
Japan our dinner arrived live in a basket from the fishing boats docked
below the restaurant. The chefs killed our supper while we watched.
Talk about fresh.

Not only does fish contain a rich source of protein, have plenty of
beneficial oils and such, but fish is practically unlimited as to taste,
texture and response to cooking methods and recipes. Nature's fast

food, most fish recipes require less than 30 minutes cooking time. And it digests like a dream.

I keep little tubs of crappie filets in the freezer year-round just in case I suddenly start to drool for a fishwich or, as seems to happen more often these days, I feel my IQ falling off a few points.

More Curious Connections

When I started this potpourri chapter of how we are hooked to the fishes, I thought it would take only a couple of thousand words. But, the more I researched and snooped around, the more connections I found. I'll wind things up by mentioning just a few other ways the fishes have worked their way deeply into our lives, our psyches, symbols and our souls.

Art. From gyotaku, the ancient Japanese art of printing inked fish onto rice paper, to the wood and metal sculptures of modern artists, to the knickknacks in gift shops, fish appear everywhere in our expressions of the beauties of the natural world. The mastery of painting fish has, in the span of my lifetime alone, matured to the point that I'm not safe at large with a major credit card in certain art galleries.

Religion. In ancient Egypt the Moon Goddess was represented as half fish, and was probably the forerunner of the mermaid. Although Greek in origin, the sign of the fish symbolizes Christ. Ichthyos was the name of a medieval hymn in which Christ is referred to as the "Little fish which the Virgin caught."

Fish have proved serviceable gods; mysterious, distant, elusive. In some ways, they represent our unconscious selves, the part of us we can't quite reach out and grab hold of. The Ottawas of Canada did not burn fish bones for fear the fish's spirit would leave and not return in the form of another fish. The Hurons had old men who preached to the fish to encourage them to bite, and I have extolled the fishes in this manner myself. The tribes of the Pacific Northwest greet the first salmon of the year with great tribute and praise, chanting, "You fish, you fish; you are all chiefs!" The Maoris always put the first fish caught back into the water with a prayer, a practice I engaged in long before I ever began to read about the fishing rituals of aboriginal peoples.

It seems that everywhere we have depended upon the fishes for survival, we have respected and honored them, worshiped them and placed them atop our totem poles. And now that we are ever more spiritually in need of them and the wildness they represent, it seems the connection, at least for fishermen, is holding tighter still.

As modern totems to sport fishing, consider fish-printed T-shirts, ties and shorts, fish handbags, fish hats and fishing trophies.

Language. Finny things swim through our communications on a daily basis. "Fish face!" is an unkind cut, whereas "He swims like a fish" is a compliment. Within current usage of American slang, a fish is one who has no chance of winning in a game of chance or a newcomer in a prison. A torpedo is a "tin fish." Popular phrases include "A pretty kettle of fish," "There's something fishy about this deal" and "Fish or cut bait."

Science. By the American Fisheries Society and the National Marine Fisheries Service in this country and independent ichthyologists the world over, fish are studied for their biology, their economic value, their role in the web of aquatic life and for their own sakes. Professional books, monographs and papers on the biology, ecology, physiology, pathology and just about every other "ology," except psychology, run to the thousands of titles.

Literature. How large the literature of fishing is, no one really knows. In the English language there are some 5,000 titles on sport fishing and maybe 50,000 titles on ichthyology. Fishing is the most written about of any sport, and of the fishes written about, trout get the most ink, and of trout, fly-fishing the most words. There are some 30 titles agreed upon as classics written over the last 300 years.

According to the Bible, God commanded early on that man shall have "dominion over the fishes of the sea," and, it seems, He commanded him to write about them as well. Jonah spent three days and three nights in the belly of a fish after apparently using himself as a surface popper. From the miracle of the loaves and fishes to Simon Peter going "fishing for the souls of men," angling is deeply rooted into the traditions of Western thought.

In *Hamlet*, Shakespeare wrote, "A man may fish with the worm that hath eat of a king, and eat of the fish that hath fed of that worm."

Does this mean the bard was a bait fisherman?

The fooling and catching of a wild creature is better described in *Antony and Cleopatra*, when the queen sings,

> *Give me mine angle; we'll to the river: there*
> *My music playing far off — I will betray*
> *Tawny-finn'd fishes; and bended hook shall pierce*
> *Their slimy jaws; and, as I draw them up,*
> *I'll think them every one an Antony,*
> *And say, "Ah, ha! you're caught."*

In modern times the good and great fishing writers are too numerous to mention, so let me simply promise you that if you begin with Hemingway and read through to Lee Wulff and Nick Lyons and a dozen other modern fishing writers, with a stop at John Gerich's for a beer, it will prove a delightful, thought-provoking and educational journey. Better yet, start with Father Izaak Walton and inch forward.

Now, allow me to wrap up this mackerel with a memory from a special time in my life with the fishes.

For the couple of years I lived on the shores of the Pacific Ocean in Southern California, I hunted the fishes up and down the U.S. coast and into Mexico, surf casting, snorkeling, spear fishing, abalone hunting and snooping around.

In those times, there were days underwater when the visual pleasures of the fish's world were so powerful I would just hang there in the kelp like some human mobile and stare and wonder at the wonders of the deep.

"Entranced" covers the psychological effect as well as any word.

Quietly studying the fishes swimming in an aquarium, or snorkeling among them in warm seas, or spotting a shadow glide slowly by as I stand waist deep in a shallow bay, I have wondered if our varied connections to the beauty of fishes and the world beneath the waves take us, somehow, back to our primordial beginnings. We and the fishes are, after all, evolved from common, water-born stock, and are therefore deeply connected to one another in the far reaches of time.

Maybe, just maybe, the emotion we feel for the underwater world of the fishes is not so much that of curiosity, but of longing.

The natural flights of the human mind
are not from pleasure to pleasure, but
from hope to hope.

— Dr. Johnson

The First Fisherman

Compared to anyone but a biblical scholar, I once spent an inordinate amount of time thinking about the Garden of Eden. I was a young angler with a short attention span and during long church sermons I wondered where Eden was, what the climate was like and whether Adam and Eve ever went fishing. I wondered if they were the first fishermen, and if they were, what manner of finny things they caught.

Did they have fishing rods?

Did they have reels?

Were they level wind or spinning?

Did they use braided line or monofilament, artificial lures or bait?

Was it okay with God if Adam and Eve fished in the Garden of Eden?

Was it catch-and-keep or strictly catch-and-release?

Could they keep crappies, but have to release the golden trout?

I even wondered if, before things went haywire with that snake and all, the Almighty went fishing with Adam and Eve, and maybe showed them how to present the dry fly. I used to wonder, on those interminable days spent warming a pew instead of a fishing boat seat, if Noah fished.

Did he fish from the ark?

Did he remember to bring the worms?

Did he troll or cast?

Did he use a hand line or a downrigger?

The answers to my questions have been slow in coming. The authors of the Bible seemed preoccupied with war and sex and sin and such. They never bothered to mention what sorts of fishes swam in the local waters, what the angling was like, or if sea-runs could be taken on streamers.

Some archaeologists now agree they have discovered where Eden was. Juris Zarins believes it now lies under the Persian Gulf, at the mouth of the combined Tigris and Euphrates Rivers. High-altitude photographs have shown the possible undersea whereabouts of Eden's old riverbeds. We may have an explanation of all the trouble Noah had when the rain started and why he built the ark in such a hurry. We may even have a reason for the Sumerian claim that their ancestors "came out of the sea." Were they escaping the rising waters of the Gulf?

Setting Biblical accounts of the origin of man aside for the moment, and realizing you can't get some religious people to sit down at the same table with the scientists who study these things, I think to understand fishing man we must begin before the Bible was written, before the flood, and well before the first civilization arose on the plains above Eden. To grasp who we are as modern, still-evolving fishermen, we must begin at the beginning, about five million years ago.

One thing is certain. Man was drawn to and flourished along riverbanks. And if he flourished, he probably fished. And since there were no flood control dams in those days, "fishing man" probably had to cope with the poor fishing occasioned by rainstorms and the odd flood. Then, as now, he took his chances.

I refer to "fishing man" rather than the old cliché "hunter-gatherer man" because it's easier to say and the term fits perfectly into this book.

Out of the Dust and Bones

Fish flesh is soft and fish bones won't hold tool marks, so it is hard to tell if the earliest known hominids caught fish and ate them. All the data suggest that Dr. Leakey's Lucy, the five-million-year-old, *Australopithecus* African Eve from whom we all most likely descended, and the other *Australopithecus afarensis* were vegetarians and did not kill large animals for a living.

They may have scavenged, but there is no clear evidence Lucy and her kind hunted. Nobody can prove they didn't fish at least with their hands, but, without the weapons and social organization required for a successful hunting or fishing trip, it is believed they stayed on the prey side of the predator-prey equation for at least a couple of million years.

The next chap on our long march to neoprene waders is old *Homo habilis*. With Lucy and her kind gone, he ranged around the countryside in small bands between two and four million years ago. His brain was probably about the same size as the average, modern-day poacher's; bigger than Lucy's but much smaller than ours. *Homo habilis* ate more meat and left tool marks on bones.

From the location of bone piles bearing tool marks, it appears *habilis* ate his meat where he found it. Expert opinions differ, but it is doubtful he hunted. Hunters go out, kill something, and bring it back. Scavengers, like fast food aficionados, eat it where they find it. No one knows if he fished, but if he did, it was probably with his hands or simple spears.

Next comes our biological father, Mr. *Homo erectus*. An unusual chap still not quite human, he first appears in the fossil records some 1.5 million years ago. There is no question that he hunted and fished. His brain was bigger than any of his predecessors, up to 950 cubic centimeters. He had become a dangerous food source for those who hunted him. He killed for a living, brought his kills home for butchering and shared the meat with others.

What others?

His female?

His young?

His, dare we say, family?

Sociobiologists argue that, since meat was shared, this was a contract between the sexes, as in, "Hon, I'm going fishing with the boys. You stay home and mind the kids." And, this, as every psychologist knows, is where the first marriage problems began.

If sharing of the meat was the first social contract, was there also some sort of division of labor, and therefore some sort of social organization?

Probably.

Remember, we're talking here about another species, not our own. Does this mean that since our biological ancestors were hunting, fishing and gathering together before they were fully human, that we inherited significant elements of our social and psychological makeup from another species?

Hmmm.

The kind of folks we are today, *Homo sapiens*, were safely up and about some 300,000 to 100,000 years ago. We know that by about 30,000 years ago our kin were living in family groups, telling stories, burying their dead with rite and ritual and had discovered the first computer. They kept track of things by carving notches on bits of bone and stone.

Since no one has proved otherwise, my theory is that the first tally marks made on mammoth tusks were to keep track of how many trout were taken on a particular fly. Dry or wet, we'll probably never know, but we know for sure the cave dwellers were fishermen.

From fishing tackle dug up by archaeologists we know that Old Stone Age man used barbed spears and the gorge to catch fish. The gorge, not quite a hook yet, is a double-ended, spike-like bit of sharpened bone, shell, stone or antler that, with a line tied to a grooved center and baited, could be lowered into fishy waters. Once caught in a fish's throat, the fight was on.

While no one knows precisely when the single-pointed fishhook came into use, except sometime during the New Stone Age, you can imagine the jubilation on the discoverer's face when he landed four perch in a row without losing a single fish. This was also when, no doubt, the first tackle manufacturer came into existence.

Language and Fishing

More than the fishhook, it was man's developing powers of language and communication that enabled him to successfully elbow the Neanderthals out of the fishing holes and push them toward extinction. Some theorists believe it was language, above all else, that gave man the high ground.

Consider, for example, that if Neanderthals had speech, it was probably limited to such simple communications as, "I'm hungry, I go fishing." Early man's powers of communication suggest that he was quite able to talk about, organize and plan an overnight fishing trip, as is clearly reflected in the following, admittedly personal, translation of an ancient aboriginal cave painting: "You get a line, I'll get a pole, and we'll all go down to the crawdad hole."

Some authorities believe there may have been at least some social contact between early man and the Neanderthals. You can imagine man-the-evolving-liar laying a wild fish chase on some poor Neanderthal looking for a crappie hole. "Yeah, they were hittin' here yesterday, but today I think they've moved upriver. You know, about ten miles."

Speculation aside, one thing is clear. We've been fishermen for at least 100,000 years, maybe even 500,000 years. We only became farmers and merchants and accountants and lawyers and such 10,000 to 12,000 years ago when, some say, we figured out the only way to get more beer was to stop traipsing from one fishing hole to the next and get down to some serious hops and barley farming.

It is an absolute fact that we have been fishermen at least *ten times as long* as we have been anything else. As a result, fishing is in our blood, in our brains, and in our souls. We are, at least in my view, just as hot for the bite today as we were 100,000 years ago.

Never an idler's occupation, catching fish has historically been a matter of life and death. Though we once fished to live, and now only live to fish, psychologically it's the same thing.

From all this still-accumulating research and data and speculation, one thing is sure: we have been fishermen since the very beginning. In fact, it is impossible to separate how we became fishermen from how we became human beings.

Psychological Evolution

One of the things we humans have always done, are doing now and will do for as long as we survive as a species, is to continually define ourselves in relationship to everything else. We have been doing this little mental trick since the very beginning of our kind and the process is, in essence, how hominids became *Homo sapiens*, how children become individual adults, and how perfectly normal people become fishermen.

The psychological journey I am about to take you on is a short one in terms of our lifetimes, but a very long one in the lifetime of our species. This is a brand new journey. Points of interest along the way come from many disciplines: evolutionary biology, sociology, psychology, psychiatry, archaeology, history, physical and cultural anthropology, neurobiology and the dead-reckoning of a handful of brilliant men and women whose curiosity and courage to travel hopefully have taken us far in our understanding of the fundamental nature of fishing man.

Let's begin with how an ordinary human being born today becomes a fisherman. Should the reader be so inclined, an expanded chapter on how to properly raise fishermen according to the latest findings from developmental psychology appears later.

Development of the Fishing Self

All theories of psychological development begin by describing a basic process wherein the newborn infant must learn to separate self from nonself. Though differently described by different authors, this process of defining and redefining the relationship between what is "me" and what is "not me" is absolutely essential to becoming an individual fisherman. If you cannot tell which part of the world is you, and which part of the world is not you, you are, as we say in scientific circles, in a heap of trouble.

Take the earthworm there upon your hook. Does it know who it is or who its parents are? Does it know where it came from? Does it know when it is food for a robin or bait for your hook?

Not likely.

I doubt that, in the silence of the bait can, earthworms ever know their civil rights have been violated. Except for human projection, it is hard to imagine one earthworm saying to another, "There goes Farnsworth! And after I told him to stick to the deep corners!"

With only a few neurons to call a brain, earthworms develop little sense of selfhood. But fishermen, human men and women, do. For example, since you are reading this book, I know quite a bit about how you define yourself as separate from the rest of the world. You define yourself as a reader. You may move your lips as you scurry over these words, but you are a reader all the same. Because you are probably reading this in English, I know that you know how to read, spell and write English.

In the bargain, I know you know lots of people I know: William Shakespeare, Ernest Hemingway, Mark Twain and hundreds of other famous folks well known to the speakers of the King's English on this and other continents. You have defined yourself as educated as opposed to uneducated. Uneducated people don't read books. Since it isn't nice to define yourself as "rich," you have likely placed yourself somewhere in the middle class.

Finally, this is a book about fishing, so you probably have one or more fishing rods stashed around the house. So, you have defined your "self" as a middle-class, educated fisherman or -woman, who has, fortunately for me, enough disposable income to blow the price of a decent fishing hat on a book with a goofy title like this one. See how psychologists sneak up on you?

Becoming Fishing Man

If I am a baby and see you leaning over my crib, you are either my mother or not my mother. If the former, I may smile; if the latter, I may cry. When I am a middle-schooler, you are either from my school and support my team, or you are from another school and support the enemy's team. More generally, you are for me or against me, an American like me or a foreigner not like me, enjoy basketball like me or don't enjoy basketball not like me, and so on.

This "yes-no" system of organizing the world in relationship to ourselves probably begins in the womb. Unless you become severely brain damaged or join the neo-Nazis, the process essentially never ends.

It is when the lines between what is "me" and what is "not me" become confused and blurred that people get into trouble psychologically. As the famous psychologist William James once remarked, probably about a man and his favorite fishing rod, "Sometimes there is a very thin line between what's me and mine."

If you are reading this book you have probably decided that, in regard to the fishes, you are after them and a fisherman, as opposed to not after them and not a fisherman. And if I were to ask you to make a list of all the things you are in addition to being a fisherman, you might begin such an I AM list as follows: I am a male, a father, a husband, a businessman, a Catholic, a Democrat, a home owner, a Knicks fan, a member of the Audubon Society and so on down the list of the many things each of us is.

Where you rank "fisherman" would tell me a lot about how you see yourself, how you value various parts of your life and what you tend to do on Saturday mornings. I can't guess where you would rank "fisherman," but I'll wager that if someone else shelled out the dough to buy this book for you, they think you rank being a fisherman right up there with father- or motherhood.

The physical and psychological evolution of human beings did not end with the Stone Age, or the Bronze Age, or even the Industrial or Computer Age. Not at all. It hasn't ended, and it won't end. Ever.

Unless we strike the Big Match and blow ourselves into extinction, we will keep right on evolving in at least three ways: personally from the day of our birth; as a species from one generation of fishermen to the next; and collectively as a group of sportsmen and -women. From a psychological point of view, we fishermen are busy evolving finer and finer yes-no categories right now, even as I write this.

I recently saw a photograph of a fisherman releasing what could have been a world record Russian taimen, a salmonlike fish that grows to huge sizes. It is very likely no one in history has ever caught such a taimen on a fly rod. Maybe no one has caught a bigger one on any kind of tackle, yet the man was smiling as he released this magnificent fish.

This is an example of psychological evolution in action. This would not have happened 1,000 years ago, 100 years ago, or maybe even 10 years ago. In fact, I doubt 99 percent of most fishermen alive today would have released that fish. And I can imagine some Russian angler looking on and later telling a pal, "Ja! That crazy American let it go!"

This is an example of a fisherman's redefining himself into an even more recent and distinct category of angler, those who catch-and-release *trophies*.

In the psychological evolution of your fishing self, even after you have decided you are after the fishes, you still have many yes-no decisions to make.

I am a fly fisherman or I am not a fly fisherman.

I prefer lake fishing or I fish streams.

I fish saltwater or fresh.

I keep the fish I catch or I release the fish I catch.

I fish competitively or I do not fish competitively.

I fish barbless hooks or I do not fish barbless hooks.

I only use artificials or I use baits.

I belong to fishing clubs or I don't belong to fishing clubs.

I fish strictly bass or strictly trout.

And so on and so on. You can, of course, fish for anything that swims with anything that will catch them. This only makes you a fishing fanatic, as opposed to a specialist or a purist. These, too, are yes-no, self-defining decisions.

I watched my father, a meat fisherman from the Depression years of the 1930s, struggle with whether or not to release a six-pound walleye, the biggest one he'd ever caught in 50 years of angling. Dad came very close to evolving into what some might consider a higher order of fisherman that day, but his mouth started watering, and he collapsed back into Pleistocene.

The idea of fishing for reasons other than to fill one's belly is a spanking new notion compared to the eons of time man has spent catching, keeping, smoking, broiling, frying and eating fish flesh.

When it comes to fishing as sport or subject for art and literature, compared to the great reach of known human history, we've only just gotten our lines wet. The greatest name in all of angling history, Izaak Walton, didn't get rolling until 1653. The literature of sport fishing did not begin at all until 1496, when the works of Dame Juliana Berners were first published. Excluding ancient man's cave paintings of fish, fishing art did not formally begin until about 1255, when the Chinese artist Ma Yuan painted a man using a rod and reel to fish from a boat.

It's hard to tell from Ma Yuan's painting, by the way, whether our man is having a good time or just doing a job. Whatever fun might have been had while making a catch in the old days was surely incidental to the mission of securing protein.

Now that we humans have marched up from the swamp and taken

our place in the supermarket checkout line, it seems we can afford to put some sport into our angling. Maybe even pure sport. And pure sport is, at least in my view, a matter of perception and psychology and something only humans understand; proof, in some ways, that psychological evolution works and can carry us to lofty places.

A family unit is composed not only
of children, but of men, women, an
occasional animal, and the common
cold.

— Ogden Nash

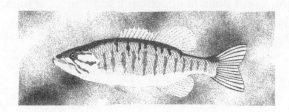

Whatever Became
of Fishing Man?

Except for a very few aboriginal peoples still living in the bush and out of reach of modern civilization, ancient fishing man is as dead as a mackerel.

Or is he?

Is it possible to change what man has been for 3,000 centuries? Will he simply set aside his fishing rod and step into a three-piece suit? Given how deeply ingrained in his physical and psychological makeup the fishing life has been, can he change? If he can, can he do it gracefully, without the signs and symptoms of distress that accompany dramatic requirements for change and adaptation?

I'm not sure anyone knows these answers, but as deeply rooted as fishing seems to be in the psyches of so many people, it might be interesting to explore recent developments in fishing man to see what he's been up to since he gave up angling full time and crossed over to selling used cars.

Out of Eden

According to the Bible, Adam and Eve were tossed out of Eden for breaking the rules. Humans being what they are, Paradise couldn't last forever.

From an angler's point of view, and assuming Eden held the honey hole of all honey holes, can we assume the following scripture meant that Adam and Eve probably took liberties with the bag limit?

"Because you have eaten of the tree of which I commanded you, 'Do not eat of it,' cursed is the ground because of you; in toil you shall eat of it all the days of your life; thorns and thistles it shall bring forth to you; and you shall eat the grasses of the field. In the sweat of your face you shall eat bread . . ."

It has to be a pretty angry Heavenly Father who tells a fisherman to hang up the rod and pick up the hoe, which is what this verse seems to imply. Having weeded gardens instead of going fishing on a few Saturday mornings, I can tell you farming isn't nearly as much fun as catching a batch of bluegills. Whether allegory or fact, the scriptures here seem to mark the transition from fishing man to agricultural man.

On the scientific side, we know that in most places the nomadic lives of fishing man ended about 12,000 years ago when the rod and net and gatherer's basket were traded in for the first plow. Everything changed, including how people lived and spent their time, what kind of wars they fought, and how much time they had left over to go fishing.

Instead of people getting together for the annual salmon runs and then separating again to go their tribal ways in small groups, people began to gather where the corn grew high and you could count on a decent wheat and barley crop for bread and beer. Water was needed for crops. Irrigation systems required the first dams on trout streams. Soon enough, the countryside was littered with permanent buildings, grain towers, farmer's markets, banks, bankers, accountants, insurance salesmen and strip joints. Kings, bureaucrats and politicians came along to keep everything working smoothly, and this naturally led to something called high society.

You can imagine a conversation between a young lady of agriculture, substance and breeding as she asks her mother if she can date a fishing boy.

Mother: "What does he do for a living?"

Daughter: "He fishes."

Mother: "Fishes? Is that all? Are you sure he isn't from one of those low-life, hunter-gatherer families who just wander here and there looking for a nice camping spot?"

In the Americas, fishing man carried on quite nicely until the arrival of Christopher Columbus. For good or ill, things have never been the same since.

From Farming to Freeways

However much havoc the agricultural revolution wreaked on fishing man and his simple, uncomplicated life, the industrial revolution finished the job. To the degree society influences individual psychological functioning, there has never been a sharper left turn for humanity to negotiate than the one we're in right now. You can tell how sharp the turn is by how many people appear to be thrown off the track.

Surveys conducted in this country suggest that well over 20 percent of the citizenry could benefit from professional mental health care. This should come as no surprise to any solitude-seeking fisherman who has spent a week riding the subways of New York City, or shooting craps with his life on an L.A. freeway after sundown on a Friday night.

Our modern industrial society does offer certain undeniable benefits, those neoprene waders I mentioned earlier, for example. But the world we now live in is not the same one in which our species evolved. It isn't even close.

Fishing man once spent most of his time with his family. He now disappears into large concrete and steel boxes for the day. He may mete out his days in an office building or a factory, at a job down the road or over the horizon. Psychologically speaking, he's the hole in the family donut. Now that fishing woman is following him into the work place, and increasingly absent as well, it is very hard to tell just where the family is, not just psychologically, but in actual space and time.

Where fishing man knew all his kith and kin and learned to get along with all the people who showed up at the annual fall salmon celebration, he now lives cheek by jowl in apartment houses with total strangers, some of whom are not even from this solar system. Except in extended, intact families living together under a single roof, none of us enjoy the stability of family life that fishing man took for granted. As a result, our experience of groundedness and connection are missing, our sense of belonging jeopardized and we suffer from diseases of isolation and alienation.

My parents took great pains to study the Quinnett and Guthrie family trees from which I came. On my mother's side, a good part of my genetic heritage stems from the peoples of Scotland, and likely the Scottish coast. These were clansmen, fishermen. Reading about the archaeological studies of the stone cairns built along those fishy waters, I learned that the pre-Roman tribal peoples of that area lived in small communities of seldom more than 30 souls. They traveled to visit in good weather, traded and intermarried, but mostly they kept to themselves and lived simple, short and, considering the annual rainfall thereabouts, quite damp lives. What took me by surprise was that these small bands of a few extended families lived continuously in the same humble village by the sea for 500 years.

Five hundred years in one place! That's the entire span of time since Columbus discovered the New World and kicked off the ruination of the neighborhood. We're talking about spending your entire life surrounded by people who know you, care about you and love you. It's no wonder people today feel out of sync. We're a nation of nomads, changing zip codes faster than we trade cars, except for those few of us locked to the land. In my own little neighborhood of eleven families, not one of us is from here. Everybody's from somewhere else.

We don't travel in bands with grandma and grandpa and Uncle John and a few close friends. We travel as singles and couples, with or without a child or two. All this social and emotional fracturing of kinship bonds probably isn't good for a creature historically adapted and accustomed to a little constancy of relationships. It shouldn't be a mystery why so many folks have so much trouble making relationships work, or why men and women who left their best friends in high school spend so much money on long-distance telephone calls, or why children can't seem to get along in a new school every fall. A wise old African saying goes, "It takes a whole village to raise a child." More and more, we're trying to do it with a single parent.

Worse, modern societies drive us to succeed, to achieve, to work harder and harder for that bigger house, that faster car, and ever more expensive toys, as if people could be replaced with things. Rather than taking comfort in catching a fine perch off your own beach and enjoying some friends and family and a warm fire to cook it over, modern man must dress properly for dinner, drive 25 miles at 70 miles an hour in a $30,000 car, have the car parked by a snotty kid in a monkey suit, and then tip a maitre d' two clam shells to get a table with a view of the ocean from which someone else caught his dinner two weeks ago. If he gets out of the restaurant spending less than half a day's pay for a fillet of fish he could have caught fresh himself in ten minutes, he can consider himself lucky, provided, of course, they don't overcook the fish and his car isn't stolen.

If you wonder why the quiet sound of a brook slipping through an unspoiled meadow under a clear summer sky gives you the feeling that you are, somehow, finally "home" and fitting in somewhere, consider where your people came from, how they lived, and how they got along with the world and each other for the last 100,000 years.

Men, Fishing and Prime Functions

Modern life gives us many things; longer life, better health, unparalleled luxuries, stronger fishing lines and sharper hooks; but not without costs. Being a psychologist, it is the psychological costs I see most often.

Some theorists have argued that it was hunting and fishing that gave the human male one of his three prime functions. In other, vegetarian, primate species, the male is little more than a semen donor. The human male is much more. As hunter and fisherman, he provided things others could not. He brought home protein-rich meat, warm furs for winter survival, bones and antlers for tools, even sharkskins for nonslip spear and sword handles. Skilled in delivering death, only he could truly protect his family from other predators and human enemies. Thus he became an integral part of the human family, and often the head of it.

Leaving procreation aside for the moment, it is these two prime functions, provisioning and protecting, that gave men their purpose and meaning over the eons we have been evolving and redefining ourselves into dry fly purists and blue marlin chasers. Without bringing home the salmon and scaring off the bad guys, a man isn't much good around the house, as any traditional woman can tell you. Hunters, fishermen and warriors have their place, but it isn't cluttering up the living room.

Although it isn't always clear who did the fishing in ancient tribes, it is likely men did the lion's share of it. Bigger, stronger, less obliged to care for and feed infants and children, it was the man's biological responsibility to get out there early in the morning and land those lunkers. Except for building weirs and driving schools of fish into shallow-water nets or helping in the easy salmon harvests, a division of labor based on sex was imperative.

We know from modern-day studies of the few remaining hunter-fisher-gatherer peoples, that life in the bush is hard. Good fishermen and good gatherers are highly respected. And when the day's luck was with one fisherman, he shared the wealth of the catch with everyone else, thereby maintaining the oldest known social-psychological reciprocity system for ensuring group survival.

Sharing the Catch

A fundamental law of human survival is this: I catch a big cod today and give you and yours a portion of the meat; you catch a big flounder tomorrow and give some to me and mine. Fishing together is more successful than fishing alone. Between us, fathers and sons, cousins, uncles, aunts and best friends, we beat back death another day for those we love. In the long run, if we share and share alike, everything will even out and our people will go forward.

This is the way aboriginal people think. It is the way fishermen still think. It is purposeful, unclouded thinking. There is no confusion about the mission and there is no debate about sharing the meat. Fairness means survival, so fairness rules. If you receive a gift, you are obliged to reciprocate. The debt must be paid, in kind, in like value, or in real help. If you want to be part of the fishing party, you smile, pitch in and pay back.

To share success of the venture is basic to the fisherman's way of life. To not share quickly leads to a rupture in relationships. I have seen it happen several times. Maybe you have, too. Someone catches all the fish. The others help him net them, clean them and pack them back to camp. Should he refuse to share the meat fairly, he will not be invited to go fishing with the group again. Ever.

Because of man's fundamental nature as a sharer of resources with those closest to him, there is no room in a fishing party for selfishness, greed, cheating, dishonesty, laziness or an attitude that says, "It's every man for himself." It is this equal-sharing, ledger-keeping, honest nature of ours that, today, creates the sudden discomfort, tension and climate of obligation you feel when someone gives you a too-expensive gift, and you immediately and sometimes quite consciously begin to wonder if, how, what, when and where you'll ever be able to pay it back.

In the first fishing party, there was no room for drones, thieves, malingerers, or jerks. There wasn't then, there isn't now. A well-oiled fishing camp is a thing of social and psychological beauty. The work is shared and the pleasure divided. Teamwork is reinvented in every fishing camp. With gossip and ridicule the oldest known tools of law enforcement, there is no need for cops, lawyers, judges or jails. Even rowdy teenagers respond to the social pressures within the closed and caring system of the fishing camp.

The purpose of a fishing trip is not just to catch fish. Bringing home meat is important, but it is more symbolic than necessary, as the new morality of catch-and-release has shown. What *is* important is what happens between people on fishing trips, especially between uncles and nephews, fathers and sons, old men in general and young boys in particular. Call it shoulder-to-shoulder intimacy or whatever you like, it is one of the few times men are together without women.

Before I offend women fishermen, let me point out that for all the eons work was divided by strength alone, the female side of culture was necessarily passed down back at camp or while out gathering berries in the woods. Several authors have pointed to women as the custodians of the gathering way, the inventor of the basket that revolutionized keeping and carrying food from one trout stream to the next, and that, most probably, women held real power as the keepers of the food. From studies of the few remaining fisher-gatherer tribes, I learned women and children gatherers bring in over half of the calories required by the tribe. Any modern, salaried, nonfishing wife should be able to confirm this if she is married to a man whose definition of self includes fanatic fisherman.

Women are flocking to sport fishing as never before. Is this some new age return to the old roots, to the rites and rituals and family traditions of fishing? Mothers who see me in my role as a consulting psychologist, career and sometimes marriage counselor, ask not whether female culture is valuable, essential and needed, but whether it can be handed down to their daughters from a day job or the board room.

For men, I'm afraid, the data are already in. There are very few ways left to pass down what's left of fishing man's culture except by taking your sons and daughters, nieces and nephews and their friends fishing as often as possible.

Fishing Man in Trouble

Except for the traditions of hunting and fishing and farming, where do boys today learn what it is like to be a man?

Away at college or in the military? Too late, I think.

On the playing fields of sport?

Maybe, but how many dads have time to play football with their sons? Or basketball? Or baseball? Not many.

At the movies or on TV?

I hope not. The portrayal of men in the media is nothing if not awful. One-dimensional macho action heroes or geeks with oatmeal on their chin, neither are possible or flattering. It is very difficult these days for a boy to find a decent role model on celluloid or TV, Peter Jennings notwithstanding.

With father away at work throughout the day, or for days at a time, how does a boy learn manliness, how to work, and share, and pull together for the common good? How does he learn what a man needs to know to become an integral part of his family, his community and even his country?

Sometimes he doesn't.

Absentee fathers are a dime a dozen in America and the Big Brothers organization is chronically shorthanded. Everywhere you look are long lines of kids who need dads. Full-time dads.

Part-time dads, better than nothing, do the best they can. The hours a boy spends fishing with his father, his stepfather, his uncle, his grandfather or just about anyone older and wiser and male are precious and critical to the process of defining the self, and I mean the male self.

For too many fathers who live life as if it were an achievement test, there isn't time to take a boy on a long voyage for a great fish, or even sit side by side with him on a riverbank and watch bobbers bob in a summer breeze. Our ancient fishing fathers would say to us modern men, "You are cheating our grandsons."

This is not to say that fishing will fix the problems of the modern family, or what's left of it, but between men and boys, something like fishing might. The ancient relationships men and boys once enjoyed with one another might make a psychological difference in both of them.

Few of the troubled men I see have good relationships with their fathers. A few have, but mostly their fathers are distant, aloof, self-absorbed and too busy to waste a day on so unimportant and unprofitable an undertaking as drifting down a river on the off chance the fish might be biting. A day spent idling along in a fishing boat with a son, and without a sure outcome or a clear bottom line, flies in the face of the modern male work ethic: Time is Money.

If we ratchet back only a few thousand years, it is easy to see ancient fishing man, his son at his side. The old man is showing the boy how to gather the bait, to tie the knots, to throw the spear, to hand line the hook and the gorge. He speaks slowly, carefully. He shows the boy where the fishes swim, in what holes they lie and how, when the net is thrown, it must be gathered quickly to keep the catch from escaping.

More important than the catch and the formal teaching is what happens between the father and the son. It is talk. Talk. Talk. Talk. And more talk. And passing quiet time together while working side by side. This is the context in which the old man's views of life and death, of God, of the stars and the cosmos are passed down to the boy. This is where male culture has traditionally been passed along and where, now, the baton somehow gets bobbled, and sometimes dropped.

Since your own father is the last man between you and the Ditch, it is important to see what he sees. But he can only tell you what he sees if there is time together. And time together in a fishing boat or along a stream or around a campfire seems to lend itself to helping us be more naturally what we are, and when we are more naturally what we are, we are more transparent and the words flow easier.

I know. I have sat around many an evening campfire while old men talk and young ones listen.

Hungrily.

There is projection and distortion in my portrayal here. I will own my biases up front, but stick to them all the same. I tend to work a bit more with men than with women, and my perceptions are colored by that. A fisherman all my life, I was raised by one and have raised three of my own in the tradition. In this not entirely scientific view, it seems to me men were better off as fishermen, at least in terms of the fundamentals of human psychology.

They knew who they were, had a clear definition of self, so they didn't sit around having identity crises. Their families needed them, so they didn't run away when things got tough. Their purposes were clear, so they didn't worry that their work was meaningless. Others relied on them, and they learned to be reliable. They learned to re-spect themselves. Because they respected themselves, they respected others. Because they had to fish to survive, they didn't fret over ca-reer paths, salary caps, or which color the new Mercedes should be. Because fishing takes teamwork, they became part of a team. And they learned the most important lesson of all: you have to give to get.

The lives of fishing man were fully integrated. The psychological machinery of a couple of million years of physical, social, cultural and psychological evolution cannot be shut off by a flip of some mental switch. It is not surprising to me that so many fishermen report feel-ing right and normal and emotionally content after a long day on the water. Or that they want to return to the old fishing hole again and again and again, and especially to the campfires where the stories are told.

When the sun is down and the flames dance and fishermen are en-circled by their family and friends, they can and will speak of all the things deep in their hearts, especially life, love and the love of life. So critical is this social, psychological and emotional communication between fishermen and the people they care about that, to anyone who thinks fishing is only about catching fish, I can only say, "Huh?"

To answer the question I began with, "Whatever Became of Fishing Man?" I can finish up the long answer here with a quick retrieve.

It is important for each of us to remember that down through the great expanse of time we have been evolving as human beings, we have remained more naturally hunters and fishermen and family men and women than anything else. This is how we have been and we should not be ashamed of our past, our need of firm footing, of reciprocity with others, of roots and family and close friends and the solitude of quiet brooks slipping through unspoiled meadows.

Compared to all the eons we've been on the trail, we only just moved from the taking of our meat with the seine and the spear to the taking of it with the credit card. As a psychologist who deals with troubled people for a living, I am not at all sure that the latter approach to something as important as our daily bread doesn't do as much to diminish us as to ennoble us.

We fishermen, I think, are lucky. Our sport can take us back to the fundamentals, back to the shallow waters where we first wet our feet, back even to those primordial beginnings we so long for in our dreams. A day fishing that quiet brook meandering through that unspoiled meadow can, however momentarily, carry even the most befouled modern man back to the natural rhythms of life and death and to that Eden toward which, in our haste to leave it behind, too few of us have bothered to steal a backward glance.

When I grow up, I want to be a little boy.

— Joseph Heller

How to Turn a Perfectly Normal Child into a Fisherman

Several years ago I was consulted by a highly agitated mother who felt something dreadful was happening to her son.

"A fatal disease?" I asked.

"It's worse. At least they're working on cures for fatal diseases."

"What then?"

"He wants to become a fishing guide."

Sometimes in an interview psychologists are required to put in extra effort to keep a straight fa- . . . , uh, maintain our decorum.

I realized that, given my lust for angling and the risk admitting this might have on a potential client, my next question had to be purged of any interviewer bias or excess emotion and delivered in the most impartial, professional voice possible.

"Walleye or salmon?" I queried.

The woman gave me one of those long, penetrating stares clients reserve for the moment when they have confirmed their worst fear, that shrinks need shrinks.

Realizing she'd seen through my professional facade, I acknowledged my prejudice toward fishing and offered to refer her to someone who played golf.

"Oh my God, no!" she cried. "My ex-husband played golf. But since you're a fisherman, maybe you can tell me why they're all so crazy."

I didn't take offense at the question.

In a matter of a few minutes, I had explained that fishermen were no worse than most other sportsmen of passion, and considerably better off than many.

"How?" she queried.

"Well, they tend to be happier, more contented and less stressed."

"They sound like milk cows," she mused. "But, what about my son? He's obsessed with fishing and thinks of nothing else."

I smiled. "He may have a case of the passions."

"The 'passions'?"

"It's a kind of magnificent obsession with angling," I explained dreamily. "You see, fishing is always rewarding, always satisfying, always challenging, always . . ."

"Just a minute," interrupted the lady. "You sound as crazy as my son. And he gets that same stupid glint in his eye I see in yours. I tell you I'm worried. He's nineteen and should be in college. What do I do?"

Clients are always asking tough questions like this. For some reason, they want quick solutions to knotty problems. Fortunately, we psychologists are highly trained in dodging obvious queries. If you give advice and it works, you get the credit while the client becomes dependent and doesn't grow. If you give advice and it *doesn't work*, you come off looking stupid beyond belief. If things really go sour, you might get sued. Therefore, the answer to all requests for advice is to ask the same question you were just asked.

"What do you think you should do?" I asked.

"I don't know," said the woman. "Say . . . what is this? If I could get him to do what I want him to do I wouldn't be in here seeing you."

Another thing they teach in graduate school is how to handle frustrated and angry clients.

Once I explained to the woman I had always wanted to be a fishing guide myself, and that there was no way I could objectively consult her on how she might handle her son's request to spend his college savings on a 20-foot jet boat, she accepted my referral to a nonfishing colleague and we terminated any professional relationship. Of course, I asked if she had one of her son's business cards, and I didn't charge her for the session.

Several years later, I ran into this woman in a department store. She lost the battle with her son and he guided for a couple of years in Alaska before returning to the Lower 48 and starting college. Unless I miss my guess, he did not major in psychology.

Raising Fishermen

Fishermen seem to spring up in nonfishing families with some regularity, as in the case I just described, but more often the child is aimed at the fishing life by its mother and father. Bull's-eyes are not guaranteed.

Though no one has ever asked me, I have always wanted to tell parents how to raise fishermen. As a father of three and consultant to many, I know about the vulnerabilities of little minds and, therefore, how to implant the sport of angling deep into the psychological core of an otherwise innocent child. As a one-time college instructor in developmental psychology, I am prepared to offer my own formula for rearing anglers. This formula also works to inoculate children against drug abuse and install self-esteem, subjects which will be further explained in the chapter on fishaholism.

Nature vs. Nurture

Are fishermen born to the sport or do they acquire the habit? Down through the centuries, people have pondered this and similar questions regarding great generals, opera singers, world-class athletes and theoretical physicists.

Dr. John B. Watson, the famous behavioral psychologist and learning theorist, once said if given enough time and total control of the environment, he could turn any given baby into a doctor, lawyer or Indian chief.

Can you start with any old baby and turn it into a happy, contented, clear-eyed adult with a love of angling? Sure you can. The research says so. Down through the years Dr. Watson has been proved more right than wrong. Except for some hard-core personality traits and the limitations of genetically determined things like height and eye color, nurture wins.

There is no known antifishing gene. If anything, there is probably a pro-fishing gene, so raising fishermen should be no more difficult than raising Democrats. In the bargain, you can end up with an ethical sportsman who loves and respects nature and holds ecologically sound conservation values that last a lifetime.

What more, I ask any parent, could you possibly want?

Start Early

You cannot begin your project too soon. Consider, for example, this fictionalized announcement from the *New York Times*:

"Born to Mr. and Mrs. Wendell P. Terry, an eight pound, two ounce fisherman. The baby angler was deftly netted by Dr. T. S. Morgan, himself a fly fisherman and long-time member of Trout Unlimited. The baby will be christened Lee Wulff Terry, after the world-famous fisherman of the same name."

There is great power in naming. In ancient times, names were so special they had to be given to you under extraordinary circumstances. Your name could come to you in a dream, or be given you by an elder, but in any event, it was your name and only suited you. It set the course for your life.

Announcing the birth of a fisherman with a strong fishing name, in hopes of casting the die after nine months of pregnancy, though, is probably too late. To get a neonate headed in the right direction, you can actually begin well before the fetus is fully developed.

We know from several research studies that a little one is quite capable of learning while still in the oven. A fetus exposed to pieces by Beethoven while in the womb will, several years later, learn to play those same pieces more quickly than others, providing evidence human learning takes place in the womb. I used to tell my classes this old story about an English woman to drive this prebirth learning point home.

There was once a recently impregnated woman who very much wanted her child to be both a fisherman and well mannered. To get the desired result, the lady read books on manners and stream etiquette to her swelling abdomen for the entire nine months of her pregnancy.

The nine months passed, but no child came. Then 10 months. Then a year. Then two years and still no child. At the five-year mark, the lady was huge and quite uncomfortable, but there were still no signs of labor. A decade passed. Then two decades. After some 35 years, the lady passed away.

When the medical examiner opened her up, he found two fully-grown English fishermen engaged in the following conversation:

"No, *you* go first."

"No, you. I insist. This is your beat."

"I'm very sorry, sir, but I believe it is your beat and, therefore, you should exit and take the first cast."

"Quite the contrary, my dear man. But thank you, anyway. Now, please, be a good sport, take your leave, and make the first cast."

This absolutely true story suggests several important steps that can be taken by couples hoping to raise an angler.

First, try to conceive the child during a fishing trip. I have no research to document the importance of environmental settings and their influence on matters of conception and eventual outcomes, but how could it hurt?

Next, because positive in utero influences have salutary effects, I cannot see the harm in the following prescriptions:

Expose the fisherman-in-progress to the sounds of water; babbling brooks, pounding surfs, waves lapping against canoe sides, etc.

Exposures to the sound of a screaming reel, shouts of "One on!" and the general sort of fishing chatter that accrues during a day on the water might give the tyke a leg up on angling jargon later on.

The mother-to-be should probably eat a lot of fish during the pregnancy.

Research has shown that both fetuses and infants are relaxed by the gentle swaying of the mother. What could better ready a child for a fishing future than easy hikes to remote lakes, the rocking motion of a boat, and the rhythmic action of Mom while she whips a fly rod back and forth, back and forth while whispering of rising trout, caddis hatches, and humming those joyful little tunes that sometimes bubble up from the heart during moments of great pleasure.

Both Mom and Dad might read fishing poems and stories to the swelling belly. As long as twins are not expected and you lay off the etiquette, what possible risks could there be?

Get the Birth Myth Right

All of us have a birth myth. Sometimes the myth is given to us, sometimes we make up our own. For example, if three guys in long beards are guided by a supernova to your mother's delivery room and happen to bring along some incense and myrrh, you're likely to grow up with a lot of people expecting you to do big things.

On the other hand, if you're in a quarrel with your parents about something and think they don't love you anymore, you may create your own birth myth. "There was a mixup at the hospital. I'm someone else's kid." Or, "I must have been adopted."

A fisherman's birth myth might include being born on the opening day of walleye season, or at the height of the green drake hatch, or in the back of a bass boat. Being named "Izaak" after Izaak Walton or "Lee" after Lee Wulff also fits the bill.

Alexander the Great's birth myth was that he would conquer the world. This expectation was laid on him by his folks, some Macedonian soothsayers, and the fact of his royal birth, and after a little trouble in Asia Minor, he did conquer what he knew of the planet. Whether kings, conquerors, or casting champions, the process works the same. The important thing to remember is that parents have a great deal to do with what sort of myth the kid grows up with, and therefore, his destiny.

The birth myth the fisherman father hands to his offspring will typically include a number of psychological expectations, including the imagined warm companionship that will begin once the child is old enough to become "my little fishin' buddy."

This leads me to an observation about where the trouble begins for half of our population.

How many fathers look at a brand-spanking-new baby girl and think "fishin' buddy?" Not enough, I can tell you. More parents put a damper on things by seeing fishing as a "boy thing" or referring to worms as "icky." If you don't think of girls as fishers from the very start, the odds are heavily stacked against any little girl growing up to love the sport. Almost all the avid fisherwomen I know were brought to the sport by their fathers.

As we expect of children, so shall they grow.

If you want a daughter to grow up to fish with you, give her a fitting birth myth. If it's true, tell her she was born the day the first salmon returned to the river, the day the big pike was caught, or the morning the ice went out of the bay and the lake trout began to hit. Anything. Use visualization to set the goal.

If you're a trouter, close your eyes and "see" her standing side by side with you, knee-deep in your favorite stream. See a rod in her hand. See her dressed in hip boots, a light green vest, and wearing a yellow fishing hat with matching trim. See a smile on her bright little face. Now see that smile widen to a great grin as a nice rainbow rises to take her fly. To get what you want, follow Thoreau's advice, "Print your hopes upon your mind."

Setting Up the Classroom

With a fishing birth myth in place, the next question is "How old should my child be before exposing her to angling?"

Very recent research on newborns indicates that, while we once thought they had poor and blurry vision in the first weeks of life, they actually see perfectly at a distance of nine inches. This is the approximate distance from the mother's breast to her face, and therefore the recommended distance for early exposure to fish pictures and fishing videos.

I'm speaking here of what psychologists call an "enriched environment." While a lot of research has been done on the possible beneficial effects of enriched stimulation, the results do not strongly support the idea that an especially busy, stimulating, enriched environment actually leads to things like higher IQ. But then again, there are no data to suggest it hurts.

Early exposure certainly won't hurt. Of all the nursery rhymes my mother read me, this excerpt from one by Eugene Field most helped cast the die:

> *Wynken, Blynken, and Nod one night*
> *Sailed off in a wooden shoe;*
> *Sailed on a river of crystal light*
> *Into a sea of dew.*

> *"Where are you going, and what do you wish?"*
> *The old moon asked of the three.*
> *"We have come to fish for the herring fish*
> *That live in this beautiful sea.*
> *Nets of silver and gold have we,"*
> *Said Wynken, Blynken, and Nod.*

> *The old moon laughed and sang a song*
> *As they rocked in the wooden shoe,*
> *And the wind that sped them all night long*
> *Ruffled the waves of dew.*

The little stars were the herring fish
That lived in that beautiful sea.
"Now cast your nets wherever you wish;
Never afeard are we!"
So cried the stars to the fishermen three:
Wynken, Blynken, and Nod.

"How old should my child be before I take her fishing?"

My advice is to wait until the child is safely out of diapers, but not so long that it has learned to sass. I started taking some of my children with me when they were but two and three years of age. If you wait until they are speaking in complete sentences you may have missed a critical learning window.

The "when" question is best answered by what I call the "set up." If you set up a first fishing experience properly, the child will have little choice but to love the sport, and here's the set up.

Only take the child with you when the weather is good. There is no point in ruining a kid by freezing her solid her first time out.

Plan to return home in no more than three hours, well before any signs of crankiness or fatigue develop. The younger the child, the shorter the attention span and, therefore, the shorter the first fishing trip.

Unfinished business tends to be remembered best psychologically. It's better to exit a hot bite and leave the little rascal with the notion that the fish are always there, always hungry and waiting for her return. She'll dream fishing dreams between trips and pester you to take her again.

Be sure the first fishing trip has a high probability of success. Bluegill, crappie, or put-and-take trout ponds, including commercial ones, will get the job done. What you don't want is a kid to get blanked and bored.

Don't buy all her tackle before you go. Once she's hooked, she'll start hinting around for gear. I know of no better way to keep a child's room clean or the lawn mowed than trading fishing tackle for chores.

"Will my child enjoy fishing?" I wouldn't worry too much about it.

The fish take care of the excitement requirements. All you have to do is take the time and make the setting as pleasant as possible. As long as a fishing trip doesn't become a time to discipline a child or work on some problem or other, the companionship, shared affection and fun provided by the finny ones will take care of any pleasure principle business.

Observational Learning

The most powerful way to teach a child about fishing takes place without the teacher trying. Observational learning, which I wrote my doctoral dissertation on, is the process by which humans observe and imitate one another to acquire everything from attitudes to casting techniques. All of us learn by imitating, as any parent who hears his two-year-old suddenly say "dammit anyway" can tell you.

Kids learn to repeat exactly what they see . . . and hear. If you operate on the "Do as I say, not as I do" model, your little imitators will copy exactly what you say and do, thus becoming little hypocrites themselves. Things like racial prejudice, bigotry and greed are learned well before age five. So are things like fishing manners and catch-and-release.

Your mother taught you to watch the hostess if you're caught at a fancy dinner party with too much silver lined up around your plate. A child learns by watching which bass plug his father selects for a lily pad situation. Every adult is a potential model for every child, and the closer the relationship between the model and the child, the more powerful will be the influence. Taking a kid fishing is a great responsibility and a great opportunity.

By observing and imitating, little fishermen learn life's most critical lessons: parenting skills, sex roles, problem-solving strategies, ethics and how to unhook and release a trout without hurting it. If you stop for a moment to think about how humans are first socialized and brought into the family of man, you will realize observational learning is the key. Without learning by watching, none of us would get very far.

Before the advent of the modern family, children were never far from their parents, or aunts or uncles or grandfathers. As soon as a boy could toss a fishing spear, he was given one. If an old man was going down to the stream to seine a batch of fish for supper, the children tagged along. Natural settings were the classrooms of fishermen past. They worked perfectly then, and they can work perfectly today, but *you have to take the kid fishing with you.*

Observational learning is fast and powerful. If you're a reasonably calm and likable person without too many bad habits like swearing in front of children when you break off a lunker, you don't need to do anything special to teach a child all the important lessons about becoming a fisherman, but you can't teach a child to fish by telling fishing stories. You must take the kid fishing. And since I highly approve of enlightened self-interest in parent models, you should take the little imitator fishing as often as you possibly can. If you don't have one of your own, take someone else's little boy or girl.

Long ago and far away I was laboring diligently on my Ph.D. in a quiet alcove of a university library when one of those dark, doubt-shrouded questions suddenly grabbed me by the scruff of the neck and threw me to the floor.

"Who," the spook demanded, "do you think gives a damn what 'ontogeny recapitulates phylogeny' really means? Believe me, no one will ever ask. Why are you wasting your life memorizing nonsense like this when you could be out bass fishing!?"

It was a warm afternoon in May when the spook jumped me in that musty old library. The smallmouth were hitting like crazy not 20 miles away down on the Snake River.

I had a big exam in child development the next day and my reputation as an academician was on the line. The existential struggle over what to do was exquisite. But I pulled through. I caught a half dozen nice smallies before nightfall.

I took my oldest boy fishing with me that day. By doing so, I may have inadvertently modeled something truly important for him, that while there will always be one more exam in this life, there may never be another perfect May afternoon to take a child fishing.

My wife, Ann, held the best counsel during the years she mostly raised our children while I was stuck in some class or behind the stacks at the university library. Aware of the risks inherent in earning a higher education at the cost of common sense, she always knew exactly what to do when I came home spiking some high academic fever or other and hot for some experiment on the kids.

"Hands off," she would say. "These are your children, not lab animals. No home experiments. Just take them fishing. You can't foul them up too much if you just take them fishing."

She was, as usual, dead right.

Fishermen are born honest,
but they get over it.

— Ed Zern

Self-Deception and the Angling
Mind, *or* Why Fishermen Lie

Many people think fishermen are *born* liars. This is not true. Fishermen *acquire* the talent. They start out lying to themselves and, before they know it, they're lying to anyone who'll listen.

There is a perfectly sound scientific explanation for all this lying. It has nothing to do with intentional dishonesty or poor character development among fishermen. It has to do with what psychologists call self-deception, a subject I will return to after a couple of false casts.

For many years, to be defined "healthy" required that a mind be "in contact with reality." As long as one's five senses feed perfect information to the brain, and this superb organ is healthy and able to make supremely rational decisions, one's life goes on without a hitch. Rational decisions, as everyone knows, lead to the best outcomes, and it makes good sense that people who see right and think right will do right. Accurate perceptions make for good reality testing, and good reality testing means good functioning.

But as a theory to explain fishermen, good reality testing equals good functioning is a miserable failure. Perfect data, airtight logic, spotless efficiency, pure deductive reasoning and cost-efficient decisions do not a happy fisherman make. Not by a long shot. Consider, for example, the steelhead fisherman.

The Failings of the Rational Mind

I live near some of the best steelhead fishing in the world, in the Inland Northwest of Washington state. I can go steelhead fishing in the most beautiful surroundings imaginable almost anytime I want to, but actually catching a steelhead is such a low-probability event that fishing reports are issued in the *average number of hours per fish taken*.

Red-hot steelhead fishing means the average angler will catch one fish for every seven to ten hours of fishing. Slow steelheading means one fish every 25 or 30 hours. Even if you fish hard all day when the fishing is hot, chances are you will *not* catch a steelhead.

Professional psychologist's question: Why do seemingly normal anglers drive 100 miles to stand in an icy river all day and make 3,000 casts to *not* catch a fish?

Professional psychologist's answer: Simple, they're certifiable and should be put in four-point restraints.

Professional psychologist's next question: How does a steelhead fisherman continue to cast all day even when he knows he is not likely to catch a fish?

Professional psychologist's answer: He lies to himself.

Elsewhere in this book I describe the nature of habit formation, superstition, and why fishermen persevere in the face of cruel reality. Here I will deal with the cognitive, or thinking, side of what anglers must tell themselves to continue to fish under such adverse conditions and why, perhaps, they become such chronic fibbers.

The Fundamentals of Self-Deception

From a strictly rational point of view, steelhead fishermen exist only because they are able to deceive themselves. Otherwise there's no accounting for their abnormal behavior. In order to go out for a day of steelheading, where the fish are few and the runs are slim, one must be able to distort reality to believe the river offers an acceptable opportunity for success.

This can be done in a number of ways, but primary forms of self-deception go something like this: "Despite the fact that no one else I know will catch a fish today, I, Me, The One-and-Only, The Greatest Steelheader of All Time, *will* catch a fish." Or, "Where others have failed, I will triumph." Or, "The odds don't apply to me, baby." Or, "I have a new fly here that will prove irresistible." And so on.

This self-talk, necessary to keep casting when your line is freezing to your guides and you can't feel your feet, is what psychologists call self-enhancement. It amounts to blowing your own horn in your own head. (When you blow your own horn so others can hear it, it's called bragging.)

Professional athletes do this all the time. Losers prepare for competition by telling themselves, "Gee, it wouldn't be so bad to lose by only ten points, or four strokes, or two seconds, or one touchdown." Winners, by comparison, never imagine losing.

Positive self-talk begins in early childhood and involves seeing oneself as special, capable, smart and completely able to do any damn thing you want to. We see this "self as hero" in little kids all the time. Loving parents set the stage, and the child struts upon it. We see it in fishermen all the time, too.

According to enhancement theory, every fisherman tends to see himself as a "better-than-average" angler. Otherwise, he would be held down by the miserable reality of one steelhead every 15 hours. As self-enhanced, better-than-average anglers who can cast a country mile, they can't be kept off the water!

In lectures, I demonstrate the principle of self-enhancement by asking the following question. "Will all the above-average drivers please raise their hands?"

In a class of 100, 75 or 80 people will raise their hands. This is scientifically impossible. Half the drivers must be above and half below the statistical average, but this little demonstration drives home the common fact of self-enhancement and why, when you are faced with driving 70 miles per hour during rush hour traffic, it is critical to at least *believe* you could qualify for the Indianapolis 500.

Now, will all the above-average anglers please read on?

How Self-Enhancement Works

As a steelheader from way back, I have thrown thousands and thousands and thousands of casts into marginal waters. Usually, I'm too early, too late, or the run is in but the water is off-color; something. A purely rational analysis of my chances of hooking a steelhead on a fly on some trips shows my odds of success are approximately equal to those of catching a steelhead in my bathtub. But I tell myself, as I strip line in for the 998th cast, "This cast is the one."

Professional psychologist's question: Does this man need medication?

Recent research on self-deception, positive illusions and mental health say that our man does not need medication. In fact, he is doing fine. Such a fisherman, in truth, may be more sound of mind that your average citizen. He has found an answer to the depressive's oldest question, "What's so hot about reality?"

Frankly, reality is not all it's cracked up to be.

Oh, you hear stories, but most of them don't check out. Depressed people, unlike happy, hopelessly unrealistic fishermen, know all about reality. Studies show that when you are mildly depressed you see things more accurately; that zit on the end of your nose, the dead-end job you're in, the fact that when you die it will probably be slowly and of something painful. Clear-eyed, depressed people ask such awful questions as, "A hundred years from now will anything any of us did really matter?"

Since the realistic and sober answer is "probably not," you don't want to spend too much time around depressives. And you certainly

don't want to take them fishing, unless, of course, it's part of a treatment regimen. Fishing is chancy, and to depressives, most of whom
report feeling hopeless, all chance runs against you.

What psychologists call "depressive realism" is not something successful, self-enhancing and happy fisher folk suffer from. In fact, I
don't think you can be very depressed and enjoy fishing.

By healthy contrast, people who do not suffer from depressive realism tend to exaggerate things in a positive direction and see themselves as a little smarter than the average bear, a little better looking,
maybe a little taller, and certainly more charitable, kind and understanding of others. Applying for a new job, they tend to overstate past
accomplishments. From childhood they remember that they came,
like the kids from Garrison Keillor's *Lake Wobegon Days*, from a little better stock than the ordinary folks in town, from a little better
hometown than most in the county, from one of the better counties
in the state and, shoot, maybe the best state in the union.

And when it comes to fishermen, the big fish he just broke off was
clearly a world record, where the fish the depressive just broke off was
probably an old car tire.

The Case for Chronic Optimism

The fact that reality often stinks does not deter fishermen. Remember; the good fisherman travels hopefully. The most successful
fishermen are chronically optimistic. They believe, and I mean *believe*,
in their bones, and in spite of the inherent uncertainty of angling,
every single cast will bring a strike.

I did not say "might" bring a strike. I said *will* bring a strike.

Successful fishermen do a number of things less successful fishermen don't. They keep their hooks sharp, their line in good shape, their
muscles tensed for the hit, their landing net at the ready, and their
concentration and attention fully focused on what they're doing. For
the truly successful fisherman, the glass is not half full. It's filling and
about to run over.

Telling yourself every cast will bring a strike is a form of self-deception, a kind of innocent lying that, over the long days of a fisherman's life, leads to a habitual distortion of reality. It is this relentless optimism that many nonfishermen consider the key symptom of the pathology from which they believe we anglers suffer.

They ask, "How can you sit out there on the ice all day long and only catch three tiny perch?"

When you smile and say, "Easy, I could have a caught a huge pike," they often wander away shaking their heads.

If successful fishermen lie themselves into optimism all day long, other highly successful people do it all life long. Consider Sylvester Stallone, Thomas A. Edison and several U.S. presidential winners.

A young actor and writer with a pregnant wife, a hundred dollars in the bank and no real acting or writing credits, Stallone was offered $250,000 for the *Rocky* script. He turned the offer down because the producer would not cast him as the lead. He believed in himself every bit as much as he believed in his script, and in his impossibly optimistic character Rocky.

Foolish boy.

If Mr. Stallone-the-nobody had dropped by my consulting room the afternoon he turned down a quarter of a million dollars, I wonder if I wouldn't have found his bubble a degree or two off plumb.

Thomas A. Edison spent two years trying to find one element that would burn and shed light without burning up and out. He kept up this unrewarding, trial-and-error activity with the same fever and persistence successful fishermen exercise in their never-ending quest for the "perfect lure." Eventually, he lit the world.

Analysis of their acceptance speeches leads to clear differences among winners and losers in presidential elections. Optimists like Harry Truman, John F. Kennedy, Ronald Reagan win. Pessimists like Adlai Stevenson, George McGovern and Walter Mondale lose. The worst pessimistic ruminators lost by landslides. Americans do not want a president who, when he goes fishing, says, "Ah, we probably won't catch any fish and, besides, the free world's already gone to hell."

The connection between optimism and positive action is well researched. Heroes and fishermen achieve improbable results precisely because they attempt improbable feats. After listening to Stormin' Norman Schwarzkopf's post–Desert Storm briefing on his Hail Mary tactic to assault Iraqi positions, you had to believe that down deep in his bones the thought of losing never crossed his mind. I'm sure if you took the general out fishing blues off the Statute of Liberty some Saturday morning, he'd damn well catch blues whether the runs were in or not.

Self-enhancing statements together with positive illusions also foster the motivation to act, and only action can lead to results, some of which will be positive. Positive results lead to persistence, and persistence leads to winning. After three quarters of lousy shooting against the Utah Jazz, basketball great Michael Jordan went out and buried Utah in the fourth. He said of his success, "The key is to never stop taking your shot."

In case you have ever wondered why the most successful fishermen *are* the most successful, it is often because they never quit. On the water from dawn till after dark, they eat their lunches between casts. They never stop casting. They don't carry rod cases because they never case a rod. It is always rigged and ready.

Positive illusions enhance hope, and hope must goeth before every cast. Is it any wonder, then, that when the fish is finally caught, it is not just any ordinary fish, but a particularly beautiful one, outsized, and a terrific fighter.

How Big Was the Monster Again?

To keep, maintain and polish our positive illusions, it may be necessary to inflate the truth just a little. Lying about the size of the fish you *caught* comes from lying to yourself about how big and how many fish you're *going to* catch. It also comes from selective attention and benign forgetting.

Selective attention isn't very complicated, but it does lead to interesting results. Since it is impossible to pay perfect attention to everything around us at once, like walking and chewing gum at the same time, we tend to *select* out and pay *attention* to those things which enhance and flatter our self-image. Who can pass a mirror and not sneak a glance and then say to himself, "You handsome devil, you." We tend to remember compliments and forget unkind cuts. If someone says our extra weight looks good on us and should help keep us from being washed downstream in the spring runoff, we're more likely to remember it than if someone jokes, "Say, is that a float tube under your shirt?"

Since we only remember that which we pay attention to in the first place, selective attention permits us to distort and rewrite our own personal histories according to the "facts" we would most like others to remember us by. We ignore what doesn't suit us and remember that which does, enabling us to revise our image in a direction that agrees with the high opinion in which most of us hold ourselves. All our autobiographies are one part truth and two parts fiction. Richard Nixon was the all-time master of this technique and raised himself from the dead more times than Frankenstein did his monster.

As the concept applies to fishermen, selective attention has a direct bearing on how big a fish was.

How big a fish "is" assumes you have the fish in hand and can measure it. Perish the thought. Nothing shrinks fish faster than a ruler. There is no uglier intrusion of reality to a fisherman excited by his catch than scales and tape. It was not by accident that the company which produces the best-selling form of this reality calls their product a "De-Liar."

How big a fish "was," on the other hand, allows for all sorts of selective attention and positive distortion. Lost or released fish tend to run bigger than those kept and brought home. At home some depressive can demand that you measure it.

I remember very well the first large steelhead I ever caught. It was the biggest fish of my life at the time; simply huge. I couldn't believe how big it was. I announced to my pal, who had never caught a steelhead either, that it would easily go 25 pounds. Had I not stopped at a tavern run by a depressive with a set of scales at the top of Steptoe Grade above the Snake River, I would still be telling people about the 25-pounder I caught.

When the guy asked how long it was, I proudly told him, "Thirty-six inches!"

He quickly said, "It weighs sixteen pounds."

I indignantly asked if he'd been drinking from his own cider jug, to which he responded by hanging my trophy on a scale. Upon reading the numbers, and after checking the scale for damage or malfunction, my heart sank quickly into my shoes, triggering a mild, but quite toxic, momentary depression.

Up to 36 inches, by the way, steelhead weigh about one pound for each inch over 20 inches. Thus, a 26-incher weighs six pounds and a 36-incher weighs 16 pounds. I hope I haven't ruined one of your favorite memories or longest running lies.

Those Convenient Memory Lapses

Benign forgetting is the other creative tool employed by anglers to enable them to keep fishing. Very briefly, the mind forgets what is unpleasant, painful or unflattering quicker than it forgets what is pleasant, enjoyable and flattering. Any mother can tell you, if she remembered her first labor perfectly, the birthrate would plummet. If men, with their lower pain threshold, could have babies and remember even part of the pain, humankind would die out in short order.

For our winter steelhead fisherman to return each year to his punishment, it is essential to forget last season's numbing water, strikeless days, rod-breaking falls, and the many and sundry miseries associated with fishing on days when sane people are inside curled up with a good book in front of a warm fire.

It is, if we hope to carry on fishing, essential that we develop a slight case of amnesia for the disappointments associated with angling. Without benign forgetting of the days you got skunked, you would not return to the same lake again and again. In fact, the "good old days" are the good old days precisely because old-timers tend to disremember the bad old days. If I have heard the old "You shoulda seen the fishin' here when I was kid" story once, I have heard it a thousand times. And while there is some evidence the fishing was, in fact, better in some places at some times in the past, there is also evidence that the fishing was often much poorer in the old days than it is now.

Consider these lines from George Orwell's *1984*. "The control of the past depends above all on the training of memory . . . (It is) necessary to remember that events happened in the desired manner. And if it is necessary to rearrange one's memories or to tamper with written records, then it is necessary to forget that one has done so." You'd think Mr. Orwell was writing about a bunch of fishermen around a campfire about to launch an evening of fishing stories.

All the psychological research on positive illusions, creative self-deception, self-enhancement, and the clever tricks the mind engages in to keep our memories fond, our heads high, our hearts filled with hope and our lines in the water seems to support the notion that fishermen are not only perfectly ordinary and normal folks but, in fact, may enjoy a better standard of mental health than your average citizen.

If, to the pessimist, the fisherman be mad, he is mad because he remains optimistic in spite of failure and in the face of uncertain chance. What greater triumph of hope over experience than for a fisherman nine days skunked to gladly sally forth the morning of the tenth?

Is this not what is most admirable about the human spirit?

The Ethical Angler

Generally I don't go fishing on opening day. I used to work in a mental hospital and have already witnessed my lifetime share of bizarre human behavior. But one opening day was simply too beautiful to spend otherwise employed and so, as afternoon wore to evening, I drove down to one of my favorite cutthroat lakes for a bit of fly-fishing.

As I started into the lake in my float tube, I asked a fellow fishing bait from the shore how the luck had been.

"Great!" he said. "I'm just going to catch a couple more and then I'll have the limit." He grinned broadly. "I just ate two, so that means I still have two to go. Heh, heh."

I didn't say anything, but I think my beady-eyed, no-comment gaze had an impact on his underdeveloped conscience. Turning away, he watched the end of his rod for only a couple of moments more before reeling in and hiking back to his camp. He neither looked my way again nor wished me good luck.

I hate being righteous, or a vigilante; simply hate it. I'm sure this fellow wasn't a bad chap, and I felt rotten for having sent a chill through what must have been a perfect day for him. Having made the PMB flinch down deep in his right-and-wrong, I was pretty sure he hated me for it. A PMB is, by the way, a diagnostic term I invented years ago that, as near as I can tell, applies to all of us sooner or later: Poor Miserable Bastard.

However you cut it, the guy was wrong for taking more fish than the game laws allowed, and he knew it. Now that he knew I knew he knew it, I'd probably never have chicken at his house. Too bad for him, too bad for me, and too bad for both of us.

I have believed for a long, long time that ethics is what you do in the dark, *before* the game warden shows up, *before* someone tells you to shape up, *before* a PMB like me gives you a beady-eyed stare that slices into whatever moral fiber holds your soul together.

Guilt, Shame and Ethics

Fishing gives the average bloke the perfect occasion to measure his own integrity. The rules are easily broken, the temptations great, the witnesses few and the justifications for wrongdoing ample. What better circumstance to plumb the depths of one's character?

Or is it the shallows of one's character?

I have looked long and hard into the nature of people and often found a great deal less nobility than I'd hoped for; sometimes more, but frequently less; a scruple here, a virtue there. My dredging failed to produce enough of that old New England conscience to leave my car unlocked in public places. It seems many Americans, including fishermen, have stumbled down that slippery slope where one's code of conduct is no longer governed by guilt, but by shame.

There is a big difference between shame and guilt. Shame is what you feel when they catch you doing something wrong; guilt is what you feel when you do something you know is wrong, period. One requires law enforcers. The other requires only the presence of that still small voice deep in the old nervous system. Both can be wrongly conditioned for in a psychologically dysfunctional home, and you can, through no fault of your own, end up feeling guilty over nothing and shamed for the wrong reasons. Still, guilt and shame and their associated emotions of fear and anxiety are the only known internalized tools for self-control.

With an operative, guilt-affected conscience, you need never look over your shoulder to see if the law is watching as you angle along a stream catching fish. You are the law. And as a law-abider, if you respect yourself, you will respect the law. This is a simple formula. An ethical angler needs a game warden like a trout needs a parachute.

Shame is another matter. To be shamed you have to be caught and at least threatened with punishment or embarrassment. Some people are able to stay on the straight and narrow out of fear of shame, but as the odds of getting caught go down, so does the effectiveness of shame. Shame works, but it takes at least two people.

Legal vs. Ethical

Being legal is not the same thing as being ethical. To equate ethics with legality is to adopt the morals of a swindler. Many of us can name major U.S. corporations whose behavior toward our ecosystems is both perfectly legal and perfectly immoral. As ephemeral as they are, ethics go where laws dare not.

We all know law-abiding citizens who wouldn't know a scruple if they fell over one. As of this writing, it is lawful to gill net on the high seas and clear-cut above salmon and steelhead spawning steams. It may be legal to take spawning northern pike while they are vulnerable in the early spring, but it's ethically wrong to take even one if the fishery can't stand it, or if you don't need the fish.

These days sportsmen complain about the complexity of fishing regulations, but without tighter external controls to protect the fisheries, unscrupulous anglers would clean out the streams, haul away the spawners, and otherwise decimate wildlife, something mankind has a bloody history of doing very well.

In a perfect world you would need no laws, just the following guideline: Enjoy yourself, but please do not harm the fishery. Here and now, to protect a threatened fishery you need either biologically sound regulations and strict enforcement of those regulations, or a highly ethical fishing public.

The fishes need ethical fishermen. More, they need ethical fishermen to defend them against the stupidity, arrogance and the unmitigated greed of the unethical. We cannot legislate morality and ethical behavior any more than we can legislate the human heart, so it is up to each fisherman to take a long and sometimes painful journey, not to the points of the compass, but inward.

Moral Thinking for Moral Fishermen

Psychologists have studied child development since the beginning of our science, and we know that it is imperative that every child in every society learn what is right or wrong in terms of their own culture. This "yes-no" system of categorizing thought and action as good and bad is essential to the development of character and the development of the self.

Jean Piaget, the famous French psychologist, began these studies with his 1932 book *The Moral Judgment of the Child*. Considerable strides have been made by others since then, and especially with the work of Lawrence Kohlberg, from whom I will borrow heavily here.

Moral development is tied directly to cognitive development, the growth of thinking ability. Ethical behavior can only be achieved if the brain is sound, functional and fully mature. You need a reasonably aged, healthy glob of gray matter at the end of your spinal column to rise to catch-and-release angling. Because of the ability to think and reason, humans are capable of moral principles and ethical behavior. Grizzlies, mink, sea lions, ospreys and great blue herons don't give a fig for ethics.

While still a tadpole, each of us needs instruction in morality, decent role models and a few shining examples from which to learn. More than any other way, humans learn from each other, which is why wise parents are on constant alert about the sort of company their children keep. Formal instruction in ethics is rare. While major religions do what they can, most of what we learn about right and wrong is like lint — we pick it up around the house. And we pick it up much earlier in life than most people think. The majority of social attitudes, prejudices, moral precepts and political party affiliations are acquired by age five or six, usually around a supper table or, in our instant case, a fishing hole.

Boy: "That makes seventy-nine, Dad. Do you think it's ethical for us to catch so many trout?"

Father: "Son, I don't think it's even ethical for us to be using dynamite. Now hand me another fuse."

According to Kohlberg, every fisherman goes through several stages of moral development while climbing the ladder to the highest levels of ethical behavior. There are steps in this ladder and each step corresponds, roughly, to an age range. At age nine or younger, the *preconventional* stage, we obey rules to avoid punishment or to gain concrete rewards. For example, to avoid a fine, we take no more than our limit of trout.

By early adolescence, moral beliefs have evolved to a more *conventional* type. We uphold the laws of the land for the good of society, and because everyone ought and should. Young people memorize the values of the culture at this time: the Pledge of Allegiance, the Boy Scout Oath, religious prayers and fishing regulations.

The last level of moral development, the *postconventional* stage, requires a more sophisticated analysis of the reasons for laws and how shared values among people lead to certain decisions, and hopefully decisions that result in the greatest good for the greatest number. At the postconventional stage, the fisherman is able to reflect on the accumulated knowledge of his or her culture, understands that there are universal ethical principles and matters of conscience that may conflict with, and sometimes transcend, society's currently accepted laws. The civil rights movement and Dr. Martin Luther King's vision come to mind.

An Ethical Dilemma

As a test of moral thinking, I pose an ethical problem for fishermen which, if the thing works properly, should throw a furrow or two across the average angler's brow. Hacked out of whole cloth on a model suggested by Kohlberg, here's the dilemma.

A man inherited a large ranch his great-grandfather had put together in the last century. Included in the holdings were several hundred acres his ancestor had purchased from the chief of a local Indian tribe. On this land was a 25-acre lake, a stream and a natural run of westslope cutthroat trout.

For all the years his great-grandfather, his grandfather and his father worked the ranch, the public, including members of the local tribe, who originally "owned" the lake, were welcome to fish. Upon inheriting the land, the man decided to post the lake against trespass by the public and closed it to fishing except for a few friends and those willing to pay $100 a day for the privilege.

A local Indian boy, whose grandmother is terminally ill, is asked to bring the dying woman a trout from "the lake of our grandfathers for one last taste." With his grandmother weakening daily, the lad wants to honor her wishes and sets about raising money for the fishing fee. Despite borrowing all he can from friends and family, he can raise only $50.

With this in hand, he approaches the owner. The owner refuses.

Should the boy sneak onto the lake and catch his dying grandmother a trout, or should he obey the law?

Depending on our points of view, our answers will vary.

"I'd be in there in a heartbeat!"

"The law's the law; the kid should raise the rest of the money."

"I wouldn't need a sick grandma to fish the lake of my grandfathers!"

"The tribe should hire a lawyer and get access to the lake back. It was probably stolen in the first place."

"If we don't respect property laws in this country, what do we respect?"

"Wild fish belong to everyone. The boy should take his chances."

"Are flaming arrows really out of fashion?"

The point is not that there is any right or wrong answer to this dilemma, but that one is willing and able to struggle with all the variables built into the problem and arrive, sooner or later, at a fully reasoned position from which some moral action can then follow. What action is right or wrong in our example depends on one's views of property rights, interpretation of existing treaties, whose traditions carry the greater moral weight, and even who "owns" the wild fishes that came to live in the streams and lakes of the Rocky Mountains millions of years before men of any color came to catch them.

The Ethically Competent Angler

To be an ethical fisherman you have to come to grips with who you are and how you make up your mind about things. It isn't enough to say, "Yes, of course I'm ethical" and let it go at that. You have to mull things over, lift up a rock or two, and take a peek into that shadowy side of your soul where, if no one is looking, you might just go ahead and bend a silly old rule a little before the sun goes down and the fish stop rising.

I'm talking about "ethical competence," a term one of my psychology interns, Patricia, used to refer to the ethical skills and qualities necessary to operate at the highest levels of ethical behavior. To arrive at this lofty place, the fisherman must undertake a task much more difficult than simply staying out of trouble. He or she has to understand that what is right or wrong is a constantly moving target, not a rule fixed in heaven. Circumstances and fisheries change, and what may be ethical and right today can be unethical and wrong tomorrow, as anyone who has fished the dwindling salmon and steelhead fisheries of the Northwest can tell you.

Let's admit that perfect ethical behavior is an aspiration and can probably never be fully, finally or always achieved. But that doesn't mean we shouldn't try. If we don't strive to rise above our training as fishermen and human beings, why bother to get up in the morning?

To be ethically competent, the fisherman needs several tools, including the *sensitivity* to recognize a situation as posing one or more ethical considerations; the *knowledge* of what responses are legal versus what responses might be ethical in that situation; the *willingness* to act; the *judgment* to weigh various considerations where there are no laws or guidelines; and the *humility* to seek consultation and additional knowledge to guide one's action.

Sensitivity

A fisherman has to recognize a potential problem with certain behavior. Until and unless there is sensitivity, there can be no recognition that an act might be ethically wrong. Take spawning bass for example. If a fisherman is not sensitive to the time and place of spawning, the vulnerability of the fish and the high cost to a fishery of killing spawning largemouths, he will not recognize that catching and keeping them is potentially unethical, law or no law.

Knowledge

Fishermen need to be smart and informed about the fishes and the places fish swim. Knowing the game laws governing your favorite stream is one thing. Knowing what the local fish biologist knows about your favorite stream, its denizens and its general health is something else again. While the laws take only a few minutes to learn, learning the true nature of a stream takes a lifetime. The ethically competent angler knows that too much wading in certain areas may damage critical spawning gravels, while the average, law-abiding angler wouldn't know a spawning bed if he was standing in one.

Willingness to Act

Once you are sensitized and have the knowledge of what is the right and correct thing to do from a reasoned ethical conclusion, you have to *do* it.

This is where most of us fail. The gap between belief of right action and *taking* right action is as wide as that between virtue and vice.

Years ago I consulted for the State of Washington's Board of Pris-
ons and Parole. My job was to recommend to the board which bad
guys weren't so bad they couldn't be let out of prison early to relieve
overcrowding. I interviewed a lot of criminals in those days and they
taught me one thing very well. Like the chap who ate two trout so
he could catch two more, most criminals know perfectly well which
laws they are breaking. The smarter the criminal, the more law they
know and the more cleverly they are able to avoid arrest while breaking those laws. The only question most common criminals ask of
themselves before breaking a law is, "What are my chances of getting
caught?" This is a perfect example of preconventional, shame-based,
nine-year-old moral logic; the logic, I might add, apparently heavily
relied upon by your average white-collar criminal, and all sorts of
crooks in high places.

Judgment

The ethically competent angler needs to have enough functional
gray matter to reason things out and make careful judgments. Where
a morally sound action is obvious, it doesn't take a genius to do the
right thing. But where the matter is muddled, confused and blurred,
and information and experience are lacking, it may take considerable
thought and consultation to make an informed ethical decision.

I recently read about a walleye tournament in which, after the fish
were weighed and released, the majority expired in what turned out
to be, possibly, a too-warm lake. I'm not saying the contest participants were unethical, but if any of them had doubts about the sur-
vivability of the fish under the conditions of the contest, they might
have reasoned that participation in that contest encouraged the
slaughter and was, while legally right, morally wrong.

From my own experience, I have always had trouble using very
fine tippets to catch very big trout. You get more takes, but once you

hook a heavy trout you intend to release, you risk its life through overexhaustion if you must then play it practically forever to avoid breaking a light tippet. Better to use a hawser, catch fewer fish, but get the fish in quickly and back to safety quickly. There is nothing worse than sacrificing a fine fish on ego's altar.

Sound judgment, discernment, discretion, wisdom, prudence and a decent measure of common sense are traits of good judges and good fishermen. The ethically competent angler labors to acquire these qualities of character. Such refinements of spirit only come from thinking long and hard about the questions with the tricky answers. Unfortunately, too many anglers have neither the time, patience nor inclination for such a troublesome inward journey.

Humility

The ethically competent angler needs enough humility and insight into his own makeup to realize that he ain't perfect just yet, and probably will never be. We could all afford, from time to time, to sit down to a piece of humble pie. At the very least, we need to know what we don't know, and we need to have the courage to ask the questions. Until we recognize our limitations, vulnerabilities and technical incompetence, we can never climb that last rung on the ladder of ethical competence as fishermen or human beings.

Oscar Wilde once said that "Any preoccupation with ideas of what is right and wrong in conduct shows an arrested intellectual development." The man was a wit, but I wouldn't have cared to go fishing with him.

Beyond the Stream, the Lake and the Sea

It took me a long time to inch my way up the ladder toward some semblance of ethical behavior toward the fishes and the places fishes live. Like most kids starting out, I thought fishing consisted of making the greatest possible slaughter in the shortest possible time so that, when I got back to camp, I could claim bragging rights over everyone else.

There was a powerful connection between my success as an angler and my success as a human being. What took so many years to finally learn, and learn thoroughly, is that it is not so much mastery over the fishes that matters when the day is done and the campfire burns low, but mastery over oneself.

Given the great and growing press and threat of an ever-expanding horde of humanity upon the earth, it will never be enough for ethical fishermen to care only about their own behavior or the welfare of their favorite fish.

Our obligations loom large. While we need to care about and fight for our favorite stream, we also need to care about and fight for the other fellow's stream, the other fellow's river, and the other fellow's offshore reef. There are plenty of ways to do this: writing letters, sending money to save fishy places, voting and joining clubs and organizations that meld the voices of many and strike with a great and fearful force.

And, there is raising hell.

Personally, I enjoy raising hell the most. I consider raising hell such an ethical, fully-American duty that I preprint envelopes with the addresses of my legislators and keep them at the ready. In case the morning paper reports the Asian gill-netters are at it again on the high seas, I can, in a few keystrokes, send a shot across somebody's bow.

In all the ways humanity has come to govern itself, nothing has supplanted the vote, good parenting or the beady-eyed gaze; the gaze that says "I know you and I know what you're up to, so you'd better shape up!" This is the gaze I gave the PMB who took more fish than his limit at the lake on opening day. Maybe the gaze helped him get a leg up on whatever rung of the ethical ladder he's been having trouble with. Maybe the gaze only made him mad. Who knows? One can always hope, though, that the next day he gazed into his own son's eyes and said, "From now on, a limit is eight trout — no more."

The beady-eyed gaze works on everyone from presidents to children. It's the same gaze I recommend parents use as they go about the critical business of installing still small voices deep down in their children's characters.

The installation should last a lifetime.

Notes on Sex, Marriage and Tournament Fishing

In the early days of the feminist revolution, my wife and I hosted a Christmas party for our neighborhood. As such functions typically unfold, the females took the best seats in the living room while the males remained standing and edged closer to the bar. So do the flywheels of our sex-role behavior carry us beyond fad and fashion.

Half the males in attendance were fishermen, and when one of them said, "Hey, why don't we all take a long weekend and drive to the Yellowstone country next July for some fly fishing?" the idea received a presidential welcome. George, the other psychologist at the party, became as inspired as the rest of us and promptly crossed the room through no man's land to, as he put it, " . . . see if Sally says it's okay."

"He's asking permission?" sneered the purchasing agent.

"Now?" asked the retired colonel. "Hell, we don't decamp for seven months."

"I don't give that marriage another year," remarked the professor of economics.

This proved an amazingly accurate prediction. Coming from an economist, this was especially puzzling, given that someone once said that if you laid all the economists in the world end to end they still couldn't reach a conclusion.

We could all see George ask Sally if he could spend a few days fishing with the boys. We could also read her lips.

"I don't think so, dear. But we'll see."

Her patronizing smile and knowing glance to the other ladies apparently assured them that while George had a very good head, she was the neck that turned it.

Less than a year later George left Sally for a blonde ten years his junior. I don't know if he's happier, but according to late reports he has since risen to high places in his profession and now goes fishing when he wants to.

Dominance Theory and Antler Size

Don't assume George is just a sub-macho fisherman whose masculinity is easily threatened by a competent female.

Every mammalian male, including every bull elk and every guy like George, spends a great deal of his waking hours trying to establish dominance over other males, especially when females are present. He may not realize he's doing it, but he's doing it all the same.

Human males carry on this work in all sorts of obvious and subtle ways, from fist fights to big fish contests to topping an evening of fishing lies with the best yarn. To grasp this fundamental activity between men is to begin to understand basic male psychology and also understand why it is totally unacceptable for a female to hand her male his antlers in front of all the other bucks at a cocktail party.

As a symbol of maleness, nothing so typifies the apparent wasteful, bizarre and sometimes perverse investment males make in advertising as antlers. And, "advertising" is what almost all males of all species do to attract females. Human males must attract human females because, if they don't attract them and gain sexual access to them, their genes will disappear from the gene pool, the next generation and all future generations of humankind. There is, from a gene's point of view, no higher-stakes game.

Sex, Numbers and Fishing

If it weren't for the reproductive strategies of males, there wouldn't be any way to account for why men are so nuts about football, basketball, soccer, stock car racing, kung fu, fencing, pool tournaments, horse shoe pitching, wrestling, ice hockey, fighter planes, prize fights, cock fights, dog fights, fighting fish and getting their name in the *International Game Fish Association Salt Water Fly-Fishing World Record Book*.

The IGFA record books are an example of where numbers are kept; fish weight, line strength, dates, etc. Numbers are the simplest, least bloody way for humans to keep score or, by reflection, reckon antler size. They are also the only way to control the self-enhanced liars. Without numbers, there would be no way to accurately measure fishing prowess with a rod and reel. Without numbers, there is no way to grow bigger antlers.

Southern bass fishermen who have yet to catch a 15-pounder can be depressed for years over their little spike horns, but largemouth fishermen in the Pacific Northwest believe they have suddenly sprouted five or six points if they land something over seven. In carefully managed British carp waters, big-rack anglers keep track of their "twenties" and "thirties," and anything less than a "wash-tub full" is considered a poor day of crappie fishing, which is to say that if you have to count your catch to know how good the crappie fishing was, you can't be much of a fisherman.

Men are more number conscious than women. Men are always asking after numbers.

"How many?"

"How big?"

"What pound test?"

"How many hits did you miss?"

An old fishing guide once told me that when a sport drove him crazy with number questions he would simply invent figures to pacify his inquisitor. To the question "How deep is that lake?" from a number-hungry pilgrim flying over a remote Alaskan water hole, my friend, who didn't have a clue as to the correct answer, replied with a straight face, "Seventy-six feet, on the deep end." On the other hand, a moose can swim, "about 12 knots." Numbers people seem quite satisfied with any number, real or imaginary, as long as the speaker is convincing.

For a time, I kept serious numbers myself. I wanted to know how many trout of what kind I could take on the fly in a single year. That journal is tucked away someplace now, but as I remember, I caught something less than 300 trout in 12 months, about half cutthroats and half rainbows. This was either a great triumph or a dismal accounting of how little fishing I did in that year of my life. I mean, shouldn't a fly fisherman catch at least 500 trout a year? Can he or she possibly be happy with less?

Who knows?

More to the point, who cares?

Keeping numbers didn't improve my appreciation of the sport, or the quality of my experiences out where the fishes dwell. In fact, keeping score was a bother and a bore. I think numbers are best kept between people, not between people and fish; which brings us back to antler size and male competition.

From basketball games to bass tournaments, big numbers translate to big winners. Even though the good anglers always "get a few," the best of the best back up their prowess with doubled-checked, officially registered figures, which isn't bad, just different. Without numbers, there would be no long-distance casting contests, no charter boat side bets and no tournament fishing.

Keeping numbers instead of fish will probably do more for quality sport fishing than any other single human intervention. Fish biologists and other scientists use tournament numbers for critical research and, now that taxidermists can ply their art without a dead fish, a lot of trophies live to fight another day after being taped for specifications and released.

Human Biology 101

This may be the shortest course in the world on the sociobiology of human behavior, but it is probably the longest one ever published in a fishing book.

I have pointed a finger at men and their sometimes silly competitions as if women were not competitive. Women are not only competitive, they can be fiercely competitive, especially now that some of the obstacles of social and cultural oppression have been removed. Still, the women's pro-fishing circuit is quite a different competitive arena than that of mate selection.

Catching a good bass may take a special wobble in your lure, but catching a good man may take a little mascara — as several single fishing women have assured me.

A good fish is easy; a good man, as they say, is hard to find.

The fundamental human mating dance is this: men pursue and persist, while women attract and select. Women resist unsuitable suitors and only date guys with straight teeth and big antlers. Guys with straight teeth and big antlers are believed to have both good genes and money in the bank. Like a new Mercedes and a hefty bank account, big antlers advertise success. A handsome fellow sporting big antlers also suggests the bearer comes from a good gene pool.

A gene is a selfish little chap whose mission is to make sure the information he carries in his hip pocket as DNA gets replicated in the next generation. The only way a gene can get into the next generation is through having sex; sex that leads to fertilization, a good pregnancy and a successful birth.

Once you grasp the selfish nature of genes, you will understand why fathers get so excited in delivery rooms when their newborn looks "just like his daddy" instead of just like the postman. To rewrite an old folk saying, "It's a wise gene who knows his replica."

If you happen to be a male mammal fisherman and your genes insist on replicating themselves in the next generation, your reproductive strategy is simple; find a suitable female and impregnate her.

Male mammals, as everyone knows, tend toward promiscuity. Sperm is cheap, so why not? Males are blessed with millions and millions of sperm, a kind of Federal Express service for genes. The key to having lots of little fishermen is to send lots of overnight mail. The average fisherman makes millions of sperm every day at almost no biological cost. From a purely mathematical perspective, one American male fisherman could theoretically impregnate every female in the United States in a single day, though by the time he'd finished his deliveries he'd probably be too tired to go fishing.

While your minister or priest or rabbi may not concur, and even though humans have obligations that far outweigh their reproductive capacities, evolution favors males who, sticking with our analogy, "get the mail delivered." Mathematically, though, the best male investment is in a single female, not in many — which is why the institution of marriage persists. Sleeping around is a gamble, while finding your one true love is a blue-chip investment.

If you're a fisherwoman, you have the same selfish genes but only one egg a month to invest, a 300 lifetime supply; and reproductive years are biologically limited. Also, once the baby is born, you are faced with years and years of nurturing and caring for the little tyke before it can go fishing by itself.

How does a female angler make sure her offspring not only survive the pregnancy, but make it all the way into size-large waders?

By being very careful about whom she sleeps with.

If you're going to get pregnant, you'd better get not only the very best genes available, but a fellow of means, commitment, loyalty and possessed of high-grade family values.

When it comes to having sex, most males want a yes. Before the advent of modern birth control methods, wise females said no except under conditions of marriage or clear and continuing commitment. Otherwise they might end up having a child every nine months. You'll recall the downside risk of saying yes too often from the case of the old woman who lived in a shoe and had so many children she didn't have time to go fishing.

To avoid getting tangled up with a loser, the female angler must make sure of her mate by asking *herself* the oldest and most critical mother-to-daughter question of all: "I know he's a nice boy and catches fish, but does he own a big boat?"

If you take this strictly biological view of relationships (which I don't recommend), females ought to be more attracted to guys with big antlers; tall, handsome, rich, smart and regular winners on the tournament bass circuit.

Since access is all for the male of any species, every sort of weird and wonderful male advertising has evolved; the peacock's tail, the steelhead's stripe, the antelope's prong, the elk's antler, the playboy's beach house, and metalflake bass boats powered by 200-horse Yamahas. Each of these ads carries the same information.

"I forage well! Look! I've got resources to waste!"

"Wondering who should sire your babies? Well, kid, you just found him!"

"This way to terrific genes!"

From the rooster's crow to the confident swagger of a quarterback, the male message is always the same. "Choose me!"

And if the female doesn't choose you? Shove the other bum out of the way.

Competition

A second method for assuring access to a female so that your selfish little genes can replicate themselves is aggression, designed to either frighten away or physically remove other male competition. In many species, only the males who win fights get the girls. Whether the combat is physical or psychological, females prefer winners, or so you might conclude from those Madison Avenue ads that use pretty girls to sell males everything from beer to bass lures.

Sometimes the male establishes a territory and defends it, some-times he drives off the competition. Evolution favors the strongest and most aggressive. While actual combat between mammalian males is rare, access to females many times remains limited to those who at least look and act aggressively. Therefore, when a hairy-chested, red-blooded American male has to ask his lady if he can go fishing with the guys, as our friend George did, how big can his antlers really be?

Imagine, if you can, one of the fishermen who have occupied the White House as President of the United States and Leader of the Free World, asking his wife on national television if he can go fish-ing. It would take the entire State Department working overtime for a year to repair the international damage, if it could be repaired at all. This is not to say, of course, that our fishing presidents don't ask their wives if they can go fishing in private. They probably do.

A woman who thinks her man enjoys being emasculated in pub-lic doesn't understand the simplest principle of male psychology. Like it or not, the perception of male power by other males is never in-significant. Wise females know and understand this. They also know and understand just how weak and vulnerable their fisher mates can be, and they make special efforts to nurture them when they're down or feeling puny.

Having logged more than 20 years as a marriage counselor, I have had the misfortune of witnessing more than one marital ship headed for the jagged rock of divorce. Sometimes that rock was one too many fishing trips. More often it was a failure of two people to nurture and support each other, and understand, accept and appreciate the funda-mental differences between boys and girls and how their needs are met.

Both sexes are equally powerful, only in different ways. It is the bal-ancing of these powers with grace and kindness that makes for good marriages.

In my work as a fishing marriage counselor, it *has* sometimes been quite difficult to remain perfectly objective in cases where one spouse fishes and the other is handicapped. I remember a case in which the wife whined and pouted about the high cost of her husband's fly rods,

in spite of his owning but two dozen. I can also remember a case in
which, when the couple's house was burgled and all the wife's jewelry
was stolen, she used the insurance money to buy a new bass boat and
motor, a perfectly reasonable decision, but one which so infuriated her
ignoramus she nearly left him for a walleye man.

Tournament Fishing

All this palaver doesn't get us around to the psychology of tournament fishing very well, but that is how psychological theories work.
They make good after-dinner talk, but you wouldn't want to put any
real money into them. You can have a little fun, though.

It should now be clear that tournament fishing isn't really about
fishing at all. Tournament fishing is about who has the biggest antlers.
The fish, measured by size, weight or volume, are just another way to
keep score; nothing more and nothing less. It's fun to catch the fish
all right, but it isn't like the fishermen need them to eat or anything.

What fishermen need from fishing tournaments is a way to decide
who has the biggest antlers and, therefore, who wins — at least sym-
bolically — the female and gains access for his selfish little genes. I
have never witnessed a bass tournament, but I wouldn't be surprised
to see the prize money handed to the winner by a voluptuous creature of the opposite sex wearing a big smile and too little clothing for
a church social.

Human males are much more sophisticated than other mammalian
males, thank God, and we don't engage in such obvious, competitive,
aggressive displays as preening, blustering, threats, intimidation, insults, or arm-wrestling in front of girls in beer halls. No sir, we highly
evolved human males have outgrown all that silly masculine postur-
ing and have moved the whole shebang over to things like bull fighting, tournament walleye fishing and teasing the dickens out of the guy
who catches the smallest trout.

From a psychological point of view, all this sophisticated competition between males is both good and probably necessary. Better fish-

ing contests than sword fights or Stinger missiles at thirty paces. It is, however, deep in the male's nature to find out who is dominant and who ain't so dominant. From our earliest days of lagging pennies and shooting marbles, we are constantly trying to find out who's best, second best, third best and so on. Once we learn this, we're content . . . at least for the moment. Then, finding a new arena like fishing, we start all over again.

Just yesterday, for example, I was fishing for pike and bass with my father, brothers and one of my sons when, just to see who could cast a spinner bait with the greatest accuracy, we held a brief contest. The challenge was to see who could come closest to various sticks and logs lying in the water.

The kid won. *Huge* casting antlers!

While the competitive search for dominance among males seems natural enough, it does not translate into pushing females around, but just the opposite. A male who has to push a female around to see if he has any antlers is automatically a mean, weak, nasty little bully and not fit for the company of either sex. The older, most powerful males, the ones with the biggest antlers, are usually the peacemakers and protectors of those unable to defend themselves.

Late in this 20th century the change in sport fishing from a contemplative retreat to a full-blown, cash-money, high-speed, rule-and-regulated form of mano-a-mano competition probably says more about the male, and now female, need for new arenas in which to establish dominance than it does about any fundamental change in the "sport" of fishing. My own theory is that each of us needs to feel dominant somewhere, sometime, and at least once in a while; on the soccer field, at the office, over a chess board, or off the stern of a charter boat. And, there is absolutely nothing wrong with this need.

Dominance as a fisherman is no different than dominance as a point guard or a pro golfer. The prestige and power that go with status and title are equally desirable in terms of establishing a sense of self-worth, personal freedom and power. Status and title usually lead to leadership, influence and all the varied and sundry rewards our society bestows on winners and denies losers; including, but not limited to, the attention and affections of the opposite sex.

The upside of tournament fishing must be contrasted with the downside. With some 31,000 competitive fishing events each year in the U.S., Canada, Puerto Rico and the U.S. Virgin Islands (according to a recent survey by the American Fisheries Society), and as the prize money grows and grows, nature will out.

Nature rewards cheaters. Moths that look like leaves. Lizards who puff up to appear bigger than they really are. Bits of steel and feathers that look like caddis pupa, and fishermen who fill the bellies of their catch with ice to make them heavier at weigh-in time. When it comes to survival, winning and getting your genes into the next generation, there is nothing wrong with cheating — which is why things like mascara, padded bras, lifts for men's shoes and toupees enjoy steady sales.

But formal contests often bring out the best in us, and the worst. Fishing tournaments are formal invitations to cheat. They give us a chance to win big, but also an opportunity to cheat big. The prize is material, but so is the prospect to beat the other guy. There is a certain thrill attached to a great con, to getting one by the judges and taking out the competition by being clever and willing to take a risk. This is in our nature.

Without perfect enforcement of rules and regulations and state-of-the-art tournament management, we are left to rely, once again, on the ethical competence of the anglers themselves. For tournaments to enjoy a positive image in the media, they need ethical anglers, people who understand cheating and see it for what it is: unsportsmanlike conduct.

Tournament fishing can help the fishes and the sport, or hurt both. It all depends how things are done and what happens to the rule benders and breakers.

I began this chapter recounting the tale of George, the psychologist who asked his wife's permission to go fly fishing. There is nothing wrong with asking your wife to go fishing. It's what any SNAG

(Sensitive, New Age Guy) would do. But for Pete's sake, fellas, *never* do it in front of other men.

And for Pete's sake, ladies, even if he's dumb enough to ask, never tell him no in front of the other guys. Tell him no in private.

Likewise, gentlemen, if your wife likes to fish and you don't, you'd better find a way to go along so that you can get along. Rule one for a good marriage is to never ask your spouse to give up his or her passion. If that passion happens to be tournament fishing, then you'd better learn to be a supportive observer.

Notes to the Respective Sexes

For men only: Men, over the many years I have practiced clinical psychology, I can assure you that more women complain of their men being weak and dependent, *non*-dominant, at the wrong time and in the wrong places, than complain of them being too strong or too aggressive at the right time and in the right places.

For women only: Women, over the many years I have practiced clinical psychology, I can assure you that more men complain of their woman being too strong and independent, too dominant, at the wrong time and in the wrong places, than complain of them being too weak and dependent at the right time and in the right places.

So, ladies and gentlemen fisher persons, let's get our timing down. Okay?

Contentment preserves one even from catching cold.

— Nietzsche

Stress and Fishing

People ask me, "Does fishing help reduce stress?" Being a savvy, cautious scientist whose ethical responsibilities include never misleading the public about health research, my answer is always the same: "Not if you're a fish."

The much harder question, "Does fishing help reduce stress in fishermen?" can be professionally dodged as follows: "That depends."

The trouble with straightforward answers about stress is that while everyone knows we all have plenty, no one seems too sure about just what it is, or what we should do about it. But it kills you, we know that.

Surveys repeatedly show that a majority of Americans see themselves experiencing high levels of stress, particularly on the job. A recent survey by Northwestern National Life Insurance revealed that one American in three thinks about quitting work due to stress and burnout. According to the same company, stress disabilities have doubled in the last ten years. Some employers believe one-third of their absenteeism is due to stress.

One of the most common complaints treated by physicians is stress-induced sleep disturbance. One of my own patients recently told me that if he didn't get disturbed sleep, he wouldn't get any sleep at all.

You've heard this story as often as I have: "Old Charley died of a heart attack. It was stress that killed him. He should have gone fishing." Here, from my point of view, are a few critical questions scientists need to hurry up and answer:

Does the act of fishing reduce felt stress?

Does fishing work faster, better and longer than tranquilizers, even if it costs more?

Will angling add days to your life?

If you go fishing, say, six days a week, will you live almost forever?

The answer to the last question is "Yes," but you have to remain single, live in a cave on welfare or become a fishing guide.

In spite of how little scientists know about stress and fishing, we do know a few things. Let me pull on my waders while I tell you more than you probably ever wanted to know about why I think fishing is good, too much stress is bad, how one might help reduce the other, and how *you* just might live a little longer.

I'm checking my waders for leaks, by the way, to avoid the stress of cold river water filling up my shorts next Saturday.

Stress

Stress is a state of discomfort that arises when your problems exceed your resources to cope with them. If the trout are being very selective and will only take a No. 16 female Adams dry fly, and you just broke off your last No. 16 female Adamses dry fly, then your problem just got ahead of your resources and you are going to experience a little discomfort — stress.

Running out of gas 17 miles from shore on a lake being turned upside down by a rising winter storm delivers a much larger dose of stress than running out of No. 16 Adamses — especially if you're in an open, 10-foot pram, the lake is Lake Michigan, and you forgot your life preserver. When you remember you can't swim a lick, you're very likely to experience the kind of raw, unmitigated stress that motivates people to reconsider their religious commitments.

Stressors can be broken down into three areas: catastrophes, sig-

nificant life changes and daily hassles. Catastrophes include war, nuclear accidents and natural disasters like floods, typhoons, tornadoes,
earthquakes, volcanic eruptions and any wind strong enough to slam
the car door on your favorite fly rod.

Significant life changes include biological stressors like extreme
heat, viral infections, physical injury and icy river water on your pri-
vates. Psychological stressors include signficant losses, rejection, damaged self-esteem and running out of No. 16 female Adamses.

A significant change is stressful because adapting to that change
requires energy you wouldn't otherwise expend.

The heavy hitters of change-related stress include the loss of a
loved one through any of the big Ds: death, divorce or desertion.
Then there are being fired; being fired *upon,* as police and combat
troops are; being sent to jail; serious personal injury or illness; retire-
ment; changing jobs; pregnancy; and, in my experience, coming down
with the flu the night before a long-awaited fishing trip.

These changes are clear, cogent and convincing stressors. The organism experiencing them must make major adaptations to remain
calm and balanced, including changing routines, attitudes, lives and
sometimes even beliefs.

Change and adaptation take energy. This energy sometimes exceeds
physical, psychological and spiritual resources. When this happens,
you may experience enough stress to have symptoms.

Where Symptoms Come From

Catastrophes. Certain stressors cause symptoms of distress. Stress-
related mental and emotional symptoms increase dramatically in those
affected by man-made or natural disasters. If we put a perfectly healthy
young man or woman in a combat zone and let the enemy shoot at
them for six months, they will probably also develop stress-related
symptoms. The symptoms may be minor or major, but they will experience enough stress to become symptomatic.

A new discipline is looking at what stress does to the immune system. Psychoneuroimmunology studies the role of attitudes, feelings, thoughts, personality and perceptions and how these interact and affect the physiological functions of the body. People suffering from acute or chronic stress may get sick from whatever bug is going around. There is *always* a bug going around, and an overload of stress may lower your resistance to infection, allowing the bug to take you down. For example, I know workaholic fishermen who, because not being at the office is so stressful to them, get sick while taking a few days off to go fishing.

Life Changes. Significant life changes, the second type of stressor, are much more common and therefore more deadly than catastrophes. If you have ever been through one of those Years from Hell during which you divorced, a pal died, you moved to another city to another a job and assumed a $200,000 mortgage on a $50,000 salary, the relatives who came for Christmas stayed till May, your dog got run over, your home owner's insurance lapsed two days before your boat motor was stolen, and your tackle box tipped over in the hot sun and the bass plugs made love to melting rubber salamanders, you know about significant life changes and the stress they produce. You shouldn't be surprised when your doctor tells you to take a good, long fishing vacation before you melt down like your rubber worms.

More than anything else, it's the lifestyles we develop to cope with the ordinary changes that kill us. Heart disease, cancer, strokes and accidents, the four leading causes of death in America, are more strongly influenced by our response to stress than by lousy genes. Smoking, alcohol and drug abuse, too little exercise, poor eating habits and wrong reactions to stress — these are the things that take us out early. Show me an obese, angry, two-pack-a-day, under-exercised smoker, and I'll show you a guy fishing with a frayed leader.

It doesn't take a genius to figure out what might happen to a fisherman whose lifestyle has already put him well into his backing and weakened his leader to the breaking point when he's hit with a Year from Hell. He gets sick. All of us have a weak spot in our biological and psychological leaders; heart, head, immune system, emotional response, what have you. It is this weak spot that gives way when we're clobbered by some serious stressors.

The relationship of stress to illness has been repeatedly pointed out by no less authorities than the National Academy of Sciences. According to the American Academy of Family Physicians, stress-related illnesses make up two-thirds of all office visits. The data are in. Too much stress *can* kill you.

Hassles. For lectures on stress, I designed a morning to put any normal human being in need of a rubber room. The type of stressors most fishermen experience are not big-ticket items but little, daily tragedies that accumulate over days and weeks and, sooner or later, drive us looney tunes. Here is a crazy-making morning just for you.

You wake up from a poor night's sleep to find your alarm did not go off and that you are 30 minutes behind schedule. Fred, your fishing partner who hates to wait, will be here in ten minutes.

Rushing into the bathroom, you take care of business, after which you wonder aloud, "Couldn't someone, sometime, PLE-E-ASE replace the toilet paper?"

You find the toothpaste tube is finally and completely empty, but not before finding out the kids used your toothbush to groom the cat.

You nick yourself with the razor and bleed on your favorite fishing shirt.

You say to yourself, "Hell, why am I shaving? I'm going *fishing!*"

Fred is only moments away, and there is no time for anything but toast. The children gave the last slice of bread to the dog.

Glancing at the paper, you notice a major toxic spill has just occurred in the river you and Fred were headed to. It's your favorite river.

The phone rings. It's early Saturday morning, but your insurance agent has called to tell you that if he doesn't get a check today he'll have to cancel the policy on you, your house, your car and your fishing boat.

You choke down cold cereal dry because there is no milk, either.

You open the fridge to grab the nightcrawlers. They're not on the shelf next to the empty milk carton where you left them. You find them in the freezer.

Fred is in the drive, honking.

You grab your new walleye rod and stumble out the door. You step on the cat, which probably had it coming and can take it. Your new rod didn't have it coming and couldn't take it. A little over half of it is outside the door you just slammed it in.

Bending over to pick up what's left of the rod, you notice an untied shoelace, forgetting the cup of hot coffee in your other hand, which is now warming your crotch more than is really comfortable.

Carefully setting down the broken rod and empty coffee cup, you get a firm grip on the shoelace and pull. It snaps.

And with it, so does your mind.

If we scientists could slap a pressure cuff on you just as you went rigid and began to ricochet dangerously around the porch, we would find your blood pressure a tad on the high side. That is, if you didn't leap up and throttle us first. We might very well advise you to take it easy the rest of the day and not develop any backlashes.

We know that stress accumulates and that any growing list of hassles and annoyances will eventually grind up and grind down even the strongest mind.

Stress and Fishing

I've found that leak in my waders and have a good patch drying, so let's put all this stress and fishing business together and get on down to the river.

Relaxing in a fishing boat is obviously better for a person than grinding molars in some urban gridlock, especially when you realize half the angry people creeping along beside you are stoned or drunk and about 20 percent are armed. Traffic jams, rude waitresses, long lines, unremitting noise and overcrowding are the psychological assassins of modern life. They can be successfully ditched on a stream or a river or a pond or out in the middle of a big, blue lake.

There isn't much we can do about natural disasters, but there is something we can do about our lifestyles and handling the ordinary stress of existence.

Mickey Spillane's not-too-bright weight lifter and health-food nut once said, "Gee, if you don't take care of your body, where you gonna live?" We can all eat a little better. We can exercise a little more. We can begin to treat our bodies like we would an expensive canoe. We only get one body, so we might change our attitudes toward it.

If you are not careful, stress can sneak into your fishing like cold river water sneaks into leaky waders. All you have to do to turn any ordinarily relaxing activity like fishing into a psychological combat zone is to leave it in the hands of two or more Americans.

Americans are notorious for not taking good advice. What can you say to a country that smokes billions of cigarettes a year while banning an artificial sweetener because of a one-in-a-million chance it will cause cancer?

And then there is The Dream. Hidden deep in our cultural values is The American Dream. As it is too often perverted, it encourages us all to work and compete like hell to achieve *it*, whatever *it* is.

Whatever it is — maximum personal achievement, a ton of material goods, two cars in the garage, college educations for the kids, a home fit for a prince, vacations in the islands, a pile of trophies, etc. — it is a very real dream and even fishermen don't escape it.

The dream might be catching the biggest stringer of bluegill the world has ever seen. Or getting on the cover of a slick trout magazine holding the biggest salmon ever taken on a fly rod. Or landing a new world record largemouth bass. Or earning big bucks in some fishing contest. Record fish, cash money contests, side bets, winning the daily on a charter boat, spending a year angling for a personal-best muskie — it doesn't seem to matter what some fishermen do, just as long as they do it *fanatically*.

Friendly competition with others is one thing; too much competition with yourself can kill you.

I've fished with anglers who thought we were trying out for the

Olympics. I didn't like it much. If you find yourself gearing up to go fishing as if you were gearing up for hand-to-hand combat, or getting short with the people you're fishing with, or angry when the fish are not hitting, you need to back up, sit down, count to ten, and start re-ordering your priorities before they start reordering you.

Stress also creeps into fishing through technology — not the success of technology, but our reliance on it and the fact that it sometimes fails us.

Before electronic fish finders became available, I could be entirely happy working an unknown shoreline by casting a good search pattern all day. No more. Without my sonar I feel blind as a bat. If my sonar fails, my mood isn't very pretty. "Aggravated" doesn't quite cover it.

Being a psychologist, I understand all this stuff perfectly well, which is why I am able to keep my ranting and raving to a bare minimum and have never hit a piece of electronics with anything harder than a solid oak priest. Just kidding.

Fishing should not be stressful. If you make your living at it, I suppose, it's okay to get all worked up over a poor bite. Those of us in it for the sport might take a minute or two to examine just what is it we were after in the first place. The best remedy for stress is a re-adjustment of attitude, not a readjustment of reality.

The waders are patched. I just need to get my vest and find a lucky hat.

Recommendations for the Stress-Resistant Fisherman

The stress of modern life is great for business. Psychologists, psychiatrists, counselors, addictions specialists are all as busy as one-armed paper hangers. In fact, we're so shorthanded right now we're all working overtime just to keep up with the demand. My waiting list is already longer than a 15-foot sturgeon rod, so let me give you the shortest short-course on stress management you'll ever find.

1. Get control of your life. Start small, but take personal control. If you're not in control of your life, who is, and more importantly will whoever is in charge of your life ever ask you to go fishing? If you can't answer this question, call someone immediately and go fishing. Or go alone. Now!

2. The human body is highly vulnerable to cigarette smoke, too much booze, high-speed crashes and extreme cold. Quit smoking, drink moderately, buckle up and be sure to keep your waders patched.

3. Eat a lot of fish. If you catch your own fish you will be twice blessed — once in the catching, and once in the eating. Don't pick up a load of guilt bending the law taking too many fish, or the wrong fish or a fish that, in your heart, you know should live to fight another day. Guilt gathered up for low and sorry crimes is, as any shrink can tell you, bad for your health.

4. Never buy new waders because you've "outgrown" your old pair. You attain your normal body weight by about age 20. Try to keep it there. "Desserts" spelled backward is "stressed."

5. Sitting around all day is at odds with extensive medical research on health and exercise. Go fishing as often as possible. Don't just sit in a boat and troll. Walk, walk and walk some more. The best streams and ponds and honey holes lie off the beaten path, anyway. Walking to them equals exercise equals health.

6. What a good patch is to leaky waders, sleep is to a weary mind. So get plenty. Americans are chronically sleep deprived, which makes them cranky. Trouble sleeping the night before opening day excepted, if you can't get to sleep or stay asleep, see a doc. Disturbed sleep may also indicate other problems.

7. As regards your fishing, per se, your multitudinous fishing toys and the invitation to complications, frustration and technical breakdown offered by the rapidly changing high-speed fishing world in which we now live, memorize this choice bit of advice from Henry David Thoreau: "Simplify, simplify."

For me fishing provides a critical kind of stress reduction. I know this because when I'm headed out to go fishing I feel excitement, anticipation and a pleasant little tightness in my chest as I wonder on the wonders in store for me. When I'm driving home after a day of fishing, I feel peace and contentment. Excitement going out, peace coming back — that feels like stress reduction to me.

Does fishing reduce stress? Does it give you longer life? My professional opinion is, "Well, of course it does. Everybody knows that."

He who does not enjoy solitude will not love freedom.

— **Schopenhauer**

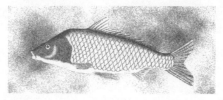

Solitude and the Case of the Jittery Disk Jockey

Many years ago a talented young man, a zany disk jockey with a wide following, consulted me about a problem I thought I knew something about. As we talked, though, his story became curiouser and curiouser.

"I'm very much in love with my girlfriend," he told me, "and want to marry her. But each time I get close to popping the question, I have a panic attack. The words get stuck in my throat and won't come out, which is a real problem for a guy who makes his living flapping his jaw. I can't think of a single reason I shouldn't marry her. We've been living together for seven months. Doc, can you help me put this trolley on the track?"

Unlike the surgeon, who has to bury his mistakes, psychologists can make all sorts of blunders every day and hardly anyone notices, least of all the patients. At our conferences we call our work scientific. When things are going badly in the consulting room, psychology becomes an art. This is called having it both ways, and it's a specialty with us.

A quick cure for the DJ lay within a couple of sophomoric interpretations about premarital jitters. I figured to trowel on a layer of standard psychological malarkey and have our boy at the altar within the month. But I was dead wrong. To get the words "Will you marry me?" unstuck from our lad's larynx, I had to turn him into a trout fisherman, send him alone down a wild river and almost kill him.

The first thing I noticed about the jittery disk jockey was that he came to his appointment accompanied by someone. This is not unusual, but odd for a man 28 years old. His companion seemed to have no other function than to tag along. When the tag-along appeared in tow on the second visit, I asked Bill, which we'll call him for reasons of privacy, "Who's your pal?"

"Oh, him," said Bill casually. "He comes along to keep me company. He's from the station."

"Hummm," I said to myself, stowing the observation away in a deep recess for future reference.

Well, a *fairly* deep recess.

Psychologists are highly trained observers, always noting quirks and casual comments by their patients and saying "Hummm." We take a whole course on "Hummm." We stow these critical data away in deep recesses of our memories so that we can, one day, make some sense of a case, provided we can find what recess we stowed that last quirk in.

By the third session, Bill's problem was as plain as the nose on his face. He had an insatiable hunger for attention. This had no small bearing on why he was in show business in the first place. He needed cheers in his ears. The roar of the crowd was an elixir to him. More, it was his food, water and oxygen. If Bill didn't have an adoring audience within grasping distance he was, as he put it, "dying."

Now that I had a good working hypothesis, I fleshed out the problem with a series of direct questions.

Did he ever go to a movie by himself?

Had he ever taken a walk by himself?

When was the last time he had spent a night alone?

Could he remember the last time he had been entirely by himself for a single day?

Had he ever spent an afternoon on a trout stream with nothing but a fly rod and his own thoughts?

Bill was horribly handicapped. He couldn't remember the last time he had been alone. The very thought of it gave him the willies. He hadn't a clue about how to be alone.

Like a lot of patients slow on the psychological uptake, Bill failed to see the genius of my line of questioning, the framing of the perfect hypothesis, and the absolute masterstroke I was about to make. When I presented my theory, he said to me, "Yeah. So what?"

"So this, buster," I said. "The reason you can't marry your girlfriend is that you love her too much to burden her with your problem."

Similar to other patients struggling to keep up with speeding psychologists able to leap tall buildings in single bounds, Bill said, "Huh?"

Bill was a bright lad, so I explained to him why his inability to be alone was making marriage impossible and how, if he would follow my simple but cockeyed prescription, he would soon find himself a whole, healthy human being capable of doing any damn thing he wanted, including marrying the girl of his dreams.

"So what do I have to do?" he asked.

I took one of those long, studied pauses they taught us back in graduate school, and then began.

"The first thing," I said slowly and in dead earnest, "is to leave this office, walk across the street to that park, and sit quietly by that babbling brook for exactly one hour. You are not to take your pal with you, and you are not to speak to anyone. And remember, I can see you from my window."

Patients will do the darnedest things. Bill got up, left the office and walked across the street, where I observed him to take a seat on a park bench by himself. He didn't last 30 minutes.

"Tough, huh?" I said when he came back.

"Impossible! Did you see me talking to the duck?"

But Bill was on the mend. He knew what he had to do. He knew that his need for people was a pathological reflection of his inability to be alone and that if he married his sweetheart he would devour her in the same way vampires devour their lovers. His dependency would suck her dry.

A quick study, Bill knew that as long as he could never be alone he was asking the woman he loved not to marry him, but to keep him alive, which was no bargain for either of them. Joined at the hip by marriage, neither of them would ever walk normally again.

We worked out a schedule of times and places he would practice being alone. He would start small. No talking with the ducks on increasingly long walks through parks. He would graduate to solo movies and meals, then take an overnight camping trip and, eventually, he was to spread his wings and take a three-day river canoeing trip on which the only allowable companions were him, himself and he.

I suggested to Bill that he might find something rewarding about learning to fish and that, while so engaged, something insightful and wonderful might bubble up from his unconscious while his brain wandered around loose from its usual tethers. Once convinced there was nothing to fear from his own mind, he snapped up the idea like a cod takes a minnow, and the cure was in.

No sooner did Bill return from North Idaho's Pack River, where he learned he was an entirely reliable, resourceful and okay guy to be with all by himself, than getting married became as easy as pie. For professional reasons, I declined the wedding invitation.

Solitude, Fishing and Mental Health

The requirement to get along well with other people has become a major tenet of modern psychiatry. We have all sorts of therapies designed to help folks in this regard: individual therapies, group therapies, milieu therapies, art therapies, activity therapies and everything from group gropes to marathon hug-ins. Read any of a number of current texts on the treatment of emotional problems, and you will be hard-pressed to find a single modern expert recommending what I did in the case of the jittery disk jockey: maybe a troubled soul needs a little time by itself; a solo fishing trip, for instance.

This wasn't always the case. In the last century there was the "rest cure," which allowed the patient to retreat, rest up, regroup and return when ready. Sounds pretty good, doesn't it?

Izaak Walton, the father of modern fishing, was not a mental-health expert, but he understood the restorative powers of fishing in solitude. "God never made a more calm, quiet, innocent recreation than angling."

Izaak wasn't alone in recognizing the wisdom of aloneness and the benefits of solitude. Some of history's greatest contributors to mankind have agreed that, as much as we need the love and affection and closeness of our own kind, we need our solitude as much, and sometimes more. Only out of solitude does creativity flow, are mysteries solved, and is grief passed through.

The Buddha and Like Minds

These thoughts about solitude came to me one evening while I was alone fishing a high mountain lake, and actually, I was not alone.

My wife, Ann, was back at the car reading a book. Ann and I split up together like this frequently. We call it the Rod and Book Traveling Club. The rules of the organization are a model of simplicity. She reads while I fish. No kids allowed, and you don't have to talk if you don't want to. The club has two members and has been running smoothly for 30-plus years. No inquiries please.

Somewhere in the woods behind me a roaring chain saw finally quit. A wonderful silence fell over the lake. Abruptly, the trout began to rise. The rings started close in over the weed beds where various and sundry insects struggled through the surface film to make good their dates with love and death. Then, spreading like raindrops, the rings soon covered the water in all directions as far as the eye could see. I began to cast in earnest.

That's when the Buddha appeared.

He appeared in my mind's eye, no doubt from one of those deep recesses. I saw him just as I had once seen him in Kamakura, Japan.

Made of copper in that incarnation and the largest Buddha in the world, he towers over the countryside. Aged through the centuries, now the color of tea, his beatific smile causes you to fall silent, even reverential. That was how I felt toward the lake and the mountains and the trout once the chain saw stopped.

The Buddha liked peace and quiet. No doubt he would have enjoyed fishing the lake I was now standing in up to my knees. Maybe some of the other lovers of solitude would have too: Jesus, Moses, Muhammad, Newton, Descartes, Spinoza and scores of painters, composers, writers, philosophers and dreamers.

All creative people seem to have one thing in common: they share a high regard for silence and the meditation it allows. As a probable result, they contribute disproportionately to the development of civilization on the planet.

Laying out a long cast, I waited patiently for a rainbow to cruise by and mistake my trick for the real thing. As I gazed at the gleaming surface of the water no fish came by. So I shifted my feet a bit, got comfortable and let my mind out to wander.

Like my patient, Bill the disk jockey, a lot of people don't trust their minds. They're afraid if they take the hobbles off, the thing will run away and never come back. Being alone in a quiet place heightens this fear, and for good reason. When people are alone in a quiet place, a stimulus-deprived environment, they are more likely to experience mind-body separations, dissociations or the feeling that they are someone or something else.

Likewise, low stimulus-input situations can cause people to see, hear, feel and smell things that are not there, to have hallucinations. Everyone hallucinates and almost everyone has had some strange perceptual experience of unreality. Deja vu, the "already seen" illusory experience, is a good example. The mind pulls these stunts on all of us from time to time. Such experiences are a little unnerving, but they are also quite predictable, normal and even enjoyable. Drug users waste perfectly good money on things like LSD and marijuana to achieve such mental states. If they would just go fishing and stare long enough at the surface of a lake where a trout might rise, they could take the same trip for nothing.

I think everyone ought to let his or her mind out to roam once in a while. If you can't trust your own mind long enough to let it go down to the corner store for a hot dog and cola, whom can you trust? If you're treating your mind okay, where can it go that it won't want to come back from? I tell all my guilt-ridden, bound-for-hell, self-punishing patients whose thoughts are driving them crazy: "You can *think* anything. It's what you *do* they arrest you for."

I worry about people who don't know what their mind will do if it bumps into a Nazi. Or a charismatic cult leader. Or some new-age guru who says that if you sit under a pyramid made of recycled beer cans you can start or stop a war somewhere. People that unfamiliar with their own minds frighten me.

I can't imagine a fisherman who solos from time to time, and is therefore on good terms with his deepest thoughts, ever falling victim to any of these goofy-idea drummers.

Therapeutic Silence

Fishing in silence frees the mind, cuts it loose. From silence you get discursive, wandering thoughts. If you just stand back and let silence work its magic, one stray little thought might grow up to be a great big, important thought. From the roar of chain saws you get fuzz balls; from silence you get creativity.

The Buddha knew this. He didn't invite his pals to sit under the Bo tree with him. He sat under it alone, kept quiet and thought thoughts.

Some fishermen know this, too. That's why they don't carry portable radios or mix casting with conversation. Some people think we're rude. Or uppity. Or snooty. Or peculiar. But we're not. We're just in search of a little silence and, perhaps, the sound of a trout breaking water, like happened that night after the chain saw quit.

He took a little midge and fought like the dickens. Pretty fish, although a little skinny. "Not enough feed this year?" I wondered.

I've told the other half of the Rod and Book Traveling Club about this business of not talking when I'm fishing and wishing to be alone. I've told her it isn't being rude, it's just the way I need to be from time to time. Ann understands perfectly.

Fortunately, neither of us feels compelled to finally, truly and once and for all understand the opposite sex. Any couple who reaches this high level of mutual understanding, realizing that the opposite sex is essentially unknowable, is immediately relieved of one of the heavier burdens laid upon the shoulders of a hounded humanity. In our view, and Ann has allowed me to speak for her on this subject, any couple having discovered this ought to go right out and enjoy an expensive dinner together.

A fish swirled again, I felt a strong tug, and then nothing. I have never figured out why I miss so many strikes. But if I can get enough solitude maybe I will figure it out. Laying out another cast, I caught a glimpse of my mind as it jumped over a distant fence and rambled up a far canyon.

The trouble with solitude is, as Will Rogers said of real estate, they're not making any more of it. Humanity is a noisy juggernaut filling up the planet. The world human population boomed past five billion a few years ago. True silence comes only at higher and higher prices. In cities, it is nearly impossible to escape ringing telephones, TVs, stereos, jets, jackhammers, sirens, horns, boom boxes and "Muzak," which was brought to this planet by pod people and hunts you down everywhere from elevators to dentist chairs.

Studies on noise and its effects on complex psychological functioning show the impact is uniformly bad. Urban people tell me the only way they can experience any sort of peace and quiet is to get in their car, roll up the windows, shut off the radio and drive, drive, drive — preferably out into the country where the trout streams are. Now, of course, they're putting phones in cars.

Sending the jittery disk jockey off to the woods was not so bizarre a prescription. We both knew he needed to be alone, if only to get on better terms with his already somewhat wild and crazy self. Being in the noise business, a dose of silence couldn't hurt him.

It is not just okay to be alone, but essential. When alone, new possibilities present themselves. Jesus was alone in the desert for 40 days. Karl Marx and Sigmund Freud sequestered themselves for days on end thinking things up and through. Albert Einstein walked alone, pondering the Big Ones — the origin of the universe, the relationship of mass to energy, the possibilities of light and relativity, and why walleyes sometimes strike short.

Psychological research on crowding and proxemics show that, outside of football games and rock concerts where people like to be cheek by jowl and don't plan to do any real thinking, crowding has a negative effect on complex tasks, especially those which require sustained attention and concentration. We also know from proxemics research that if their personal space is violated, people get anxious, irritable and increasingly aggressive; which is why you don't want to move in too close to the guy catching all the fish next to you.

Proper social distance varies from culture to culture, but Americans need more than most. Men need more space than women and, unless I miss my guess, a Western trout fisherman needs more than just about anybody.

Speaking of which, trout were rising to my left and right. I dropped a fly between them. There. A nice fish taken in a loud splash. But not too loud.

There's no one here to experience this very nice trout except me — which is just fine. I am totally alone for the first time in days.

Relationships, Relationships, Relationships

Relationships are fine and dandy but, in my view, vastly overrated as a cure-all for what ails some of us some of the time. We trouble ourselves with relationship questions.

Can you make relationships?

Can you keep them?

Can you nurture them?

Are you sick or neurotic if you don't have plenty?

Why do you get into rotten ones?

Why do men who love women too much fall for women who hate men too much?

We never stop talking about relationships. Some say if you don't have lots of healthy relationships and a constant source of social support there must be something dreadfully wrong with you and you should join a therapy group.

Nonsense. What's wrong with being alone once in a while? It's okay to be alone. It may be vital.

From time to time, fishing alone in some forgotten back country, I will spot another lone fisherman. Brainwashed by pop psychologists too, the first question that leaps to mind is, "Why is this guy alone?"

"What's wrong that he doesn't have a pal, or a wife, or a kid with him?"

"Gee," I wonder, "did all the people close to him die in a plane crash?"

"Is he depressed?"

"Is he too weird for company?"

Then I realize that I, too, am alone. If he's like me, maybe he'd just as soon not know I'm here and feel obliged to engage in some silly social intercourse.

"Hi! How you doin'?"

"Fine. And you?"

"Good. Catchin' any?"

Etc.

Sometimes when I see another angler way out in the sticks, I just duck behind some bushes and let the stranger fish by. Or cut around some woods and get a mile between us, like I'd hope he would do for me.

I ask you, who's weird here?

I know I'm weird, I almost pride myself on it. As a psychologist, I am licensed to be weird. I've worked on my weird factor. It doesn't bother me when people wonder what sort of loner I might be. I stopped explaining my singularity to strangers when I was about 21 years old. It was a great relief, and I highly recommend it. The minute you stop wondering what people might be wondering about you, you free right up.

Now, when I'm flying or caught in tight quarters with strangers and the person next to me wants to chat and I don't, I can pinch off a talker most any time with one or two quick self-disclosures. Thanks to the popularity of TV talk shows, the psychologist ploy doesn't work the way it used to. Folks are fond of psychologists nowadays and don't hesitate to tell you about their ruined relationships, troubled kids, private sex lives and personal forms of madness. Sitting on a crowded 747, total strangers open up about anything from stress-diarrhea to suicide plans. Sometimes, against my better nature, I'm tempted to lie and tell them I'm a life insurance salesman or a mortician.

Bang! Another good trout brought me back to my quiet lake. He wasn't strong enough to strip line, but he still put up a good tussle, and I let out a small squeal. "Yyyeeeeaaaahhhh!!"

Strong fish cause me to squeal, but I try never to squeal loud enough to disturb another fisherman. I once hooked a huge steelhead on a fly with three strangers standing in the same pool and got a hernia the size of a grapefruit from stifling the squeal that fish deserved. I don't like, very much, the blowhards that shout "ONE ON!" every time they get a hookup, but I understand the squeal perfectly.

I do enjoy relationships, conversations. and fishing with people I know and love, and strangers too. I enjoy all these things. But you can overdose on even a good thing. Many folks are like Bill, the jittery disk jockey, believing that without people in constant orbit around them they will surely die.

People, and especially men, kill themselves over busted relationships. You see the stories in the newspapers. I try to stop them in my office. Men are prone to say, "I can't live without you."

I say, "Nonsense!"

People live without people all the time. They may not like it, but they do it. After all, going several months without a relationship is not the same thing as going several months without getting fast to a good fish. Of course, this is easy to say for a guy who has enjoyed the solid love of the same woman for better than 30 years.

The sun was finally down. The trout had almost stopped rising. In the little solitude I enjoyed I didn't come up with the meaning of life, the origin of the cosmos, or why walleyes sometimes strike short, but I didn't gather any wool either.

Hiking back to the car and Ann after being alone for a couple of hours, and, at other times, several days, I often wonder if it isn't the respite provided by solitude that makes relationships possible in the first place and cause, as they say, the heart to grow fonder.

A solo fishing trip gives me a beautiful place in which to be quiet and reverent, to relax and think. It also provides the precious time I need to reach down deep and savor the sweet love of the life I have, the life I've had, and the life still before me. What more can any man ask?

. . . you will search far to find a fisherman to admit that a taste for fishing, like a taste for liquor, must be governed lest it come to possess its possessor.

— **Sparse Grey Hackle**

Fishaholism

"Hi. My name is Paul. I'm a fishaholic. I admit I am powerless over fishing and that my life has become unmanageable."

Don't laugh. Some anglers could benefit from a Fishaholics Anonymous. Some say I might. You might, too. For those anglers worried about their fishing, here's a quick test to determine if you're in trouble.

1. Does your spouse ever complain that you are fishing too much?
2. Do you have difficulty limiting your fishing to certain times of the day or to certain places?
3. Do you claim that you can stop fishing any time you want to?
4. Do you sometimes feel guilty about your fishing?
5. Do you ever fish before noon?
6. Have you ever been told you have a fishing problem?
7. Do you often wish you could keep fishing after your friends say they have had enough?
8. Have you ever sought help about your fishing? From a guide, for example?
9. Do you keep a fishing rod stashed in a secret place so that you can go fishing whenever you really need to?
10. Have you ever lied about your fishing? Are you lying now?

Give yourself one point for every "yes" answer. If you scored between four and seven on this test, you're a middle-stage fishaholic. If you scored more than seven, you're a late-stage fishaholic and should consider a self-help program like Fishaholics Anonymous.

But of course you won't.

How do I know? I'm a late-stager myself and I can't quit either.

And I'm sure I never will. Fishing gives me far too much pleasure. Someone once said that all things really pleasurable are either fattening or sinful. Nonsense. The person who said this was not a fisherman.

There is no Fishaholics Anonymous, but I suppose one day there could be. America is addicted to addiction. Alcoholics Anonymous, Overeaters Anonymous, Narcotics Anonymous, Shoplifters Anonymous, Gamblers Anonymous, Smokers Anonymous and Spenders Anonymous are only a starting list.

Fishaholics Anonymous could fit right in, but it won't. Why? Give me a couple of minutes to get this backlash out of my reel and I'll tell you.

Fishing: A Positive Addiction

I have spent the last two decades as the director of a drug treatment center, among other things. As a consultant to several inpatient alcohol facilities during those same years, I have seen hundreds of addicted folks and I suppose I know as much about chemical dependency as your average bartender, and possibly a little more. I certainly know more than I ever wanted to know.

One thing, I know for certain. Buddha remarked some time ago that life is suffering. Addiction is what people do instead of suffering. Some even abuse drugs and alcohol to avoid the *fear* of suffering.

I have observed over the years of working with addicts and alcoholics who *used* to go fishing that addiction is also what people do instead of fishing. I can't recall a single out-of-control, chemically dependent alcoholic or addict who had either the time or the inclination to go fishing.

Where serious drug and alcohol abuse enter in, fishing goes out. Cocaine snorters wouldn't dream of wasting the price of a weekend high on a beautiful new fly rod. Heroin addicts haven't the energy to fish. Marijuana users are too laid back to lay out a cast. Drinking alcoholics can't get past the bottle to the bass.

There, my line's untangled. Now, where is that can of worms?

Currently there is a popular drug-prevention program called "Hooked on Fishing — Not on Drugs." Started by the Future Fisherman Foundation with the help of the U.S. Department of Education, the U.S. Fish and Wildlife Service, the American Fishing Tackle Manufacturers Association, the Aquatic Resources Education Council and the Harrison County, West Virginia, School District, this may be the most exciting drug-prevention effort ever devised for schools and communities.

This highly praised program offers a complete kindergarten-through-12th-grade teacher's guide containing activities and lessons for kids of any age. The goals are simple: hook kids on a healthy, lifetime sport that teaches the principles of conservation, sportsmanship, ethical behavior and also reduces stress while it enhances relationships with others.

The idea for the whole endeavor was put forth by a 14-year-old named Matthew Deakins who said he was too busy fishing to fool around with drugs. Fishing gave him time to "think things out," and Matthew thought fishing might help other kids stay off drugs.

I like this campaign. Our schools offer only so many slots on the basketball and football teams, only a few kids play in the band, and only a few of the very cutest make the cheerleading squad. Between the handful of attention-getting star performers at the top and the attention-seeking troublemakers at the bottom lay the great majority of children who pass through our schools, those without much recognition, attention, purpose or passion. In some ways, these are our most at-risk children for drug experimentation, abuse and eventual addiction.

Fish don't care if you're talented or in a wheelchair or blind or skinny or fat or tall or short or even what color you are. Fishing can be instantly rewarding for *any* kid. Angling gives everyone a level playing field and an equal chance to catch the "big one."

Fostering family togetherness and respect for the environment, a program like "Hooked on Fishing — Not on Drugs" offers the potential of a wonderful remedy to one of our nation's greatest heartaches, which is why I recommend it.

Catching a fish will not produce a high equal to or better than crack cocaine, but the *process* by which you "hook" a kid on fishing involves something which drugs can never replace or become a substitute for: a positive relationship with another human being. It is this relationship, not fishing per se, that can save a kid.

The only thing more powerful than drugs and booze is love. I mean love between two people not necessarily of the opposite sex. Call it what you will: love of mankind, fraternal love, parental love; I'm talking about the love that develops between people in the context of a thoughtful, caring, helpful and sharing relationship.

It's this love that does the fundamental psychological work of building decent, happy, nonaddicted human beings. If this relationship, and the love it bears, can be developed in a fishing boat, and I think it can, so much the better.

The single biggest reason young people put ruinous drugs into their own bodies again and again and again is that they don't like themselves very much. When they *really* don't like themselves, they sometimes overdose and die.

Can sportfishing impact this all-too-common American tragedy?

I think it can, because fishing can become a positive addiction, and a positive addiction does not kill you. You may have trouble controlling how often you go fishing, or be too compulsive about hook sharpness, or lie about the big one that got away, but it isn't like you're destroying your liver, brain, family and friends by putting toxins inside your skin instead of leaving them outside your body where they belong. But to take good care of yourself requires positive self-esteem — a subject I'll tell you about right after I bait up.

Fishing and Self-Esteem

To get a good right-hand grip on the subject here, consider the following dictionary definitions.

> **self** (self) *n*. **1:** the total essence of being of a person; the indi-
> vidual **2:** those affective, cognitive and spiritual qualities that
> distinguish one person from another; individuality **3:** a person's
> awareness of his own being or identity; consciousness; ego
> **esteem** (es•teem) *tr.v.* **1:** to set a high value on, regard highly
> and prize accordingly **2:** to view as; consider **3:** appraise
> **self-esteem** (self-es•teem) *n*. **1:** one's assessment of the extent
> to which one is lovable and capable **2:** a confidence and sat-
> isfaction with self

The first order of love and life is to love your own life. To love your
own life, someone has to help you see your life as lovable and worthy. In spite of the grief you sometimes cause others, someone has to
believe in you and treat you like you're a basically good kid. This is
your parents' job.

If your parents do a good job, you'll probably like yourself in spite
of your failings, your big nose, the 20 extra pounds you put on, and
the annoying habit you have of laughing too loud at the movies. Loving ourselves allows us to overlook and forgive the ordinary imper-
fections that came with the original packaging, like my slightly
crooked nose, for example.

More importantly, loving ourselves allows us to accept and love
others for what they are, ordinary human beings just like us.

Too many of us grew up in families where *being* a human being was
not enough. You had to *do* something to be approved of or liked.
Praise, approval and even love were made contingent on what we *did*,
not what we *were*. The result of this program, what I like to call Parenting for Success, is that while you think you are raising a human
being, you are actually raising a human *doing*.

Human doings are quite different creatures from human beings.

Human doings don't like themselves very much unless they've just done something — like breaking the high school record for the 100-yard dash, winning the spelling bee, or catching the biggest fish in Blue Lake. Mom and Dad only liked them when they had done something pretty spectacular, something that made *them* look good.

Recently I saw a man in my practice who was a father of three, a research physician and, by all rights, a very successful fellow. He said, "I don't know who I am. I don't even know how I feel. I think I hate myself. I'm not even sure I want to be a doctor."

This good young doctor is a prime example of a human doing. He grew up in a family where only straight A's were acceptable. If he didn't leap a tall building about once a week, his folks didn't have much time for him. Neither parent ever hugged him, or asked him how he felt, or comforted him when his heart was breaking, or ever inquired of him just what he would really like to be when he grew up. They never once asked after his true feelings and they never have. He is in his mid-30s now.

"Just once," he said to me, weeping bitter tears, "I would like my father to ask me what it feels like to be a father."

In his father's value system, the only thing that counted was winning at football, baseball, basketball, golf. Any sport was okay as long as the competition was keen and there was a chance of bettering the other guy. He just wasn't going to grow up to be a man unless he beat some other fellow's brains out on the playing field.

His father never took him fishing. It was not competitive enough. Besides, he was too busy. And, it's not that fishing would have fixed everything, but you never know.

Not surprisingly, his father's dream had been for his son to be a professional athlete. We can only imagine what went through his father's head when our patient announced he was quitting high school football so he could take an afternoon chemistry lab in preparation for a career in medicine. His mother, who wanted him to be a minister, probably had her heart broken the same day.

Then our little human doing plowed into the books, got straight

A's right through the end of high school, right through college, and right through medical school. He spent so much time on the honor roll he forgot to go fishing or find his true self. Then, all dressed up with no place to go, he ended up sitting in my office with tears streaming down his cheeks trying to decide if he even liked himself, his profession, or his life — which is why and how he got hooked on his own narcotics.

While our doctor was awfully good at doing, he wasn't worth a damn at being, because when he had to "just be" he got nervous as the dickens and felt terrible inside. Then he began to take little pills from his own medicine cabinet to ease the suffering and that's how he got addicted.

Until he began his recovery, the very idea of sitting on some riverbank watching a bobber and not really caring too much if it goes under or not was pretty much unthinkable for him. Waste the time? Take an inward glance? No way! Better to keep busy and hate the people who made him that way.

Kahlil Gibran, the poet and philosopher, said all that needed to be said about raising children for themselves:

> *Your children are not your children.*
> *They are the sons and daughters of*
> *Life's longing for itself.*
> *They come through you but not from you,*
> *And though they are with you they belong*
> *not to you,*
> *You may give them love but not*
> *your thoughts,*
> *For they have their own thoughts.*
> *You may house their bodies but not their souls,*
> *For their souls dwell in the house of tomorrow,*
> *which you cannot visit, not even in your dreams.*
> *You may strive to be like them, but seek not to*
> *make them like you.*

I don't know if Gibran was a fisherman, but he thinks like one. If you think of this poet's wisdom while teaching a child to fish, you will see how and why it is that a child, being cherished for nothing more than being there with you in nature, may begin to feel that he or she is unique and valuable and deserving of esteem; yours and his or her own.

As companions to adults, kids begin to see themselves as individuals to talk with, to joke with, to eat with, to catch fish with and to share the joys and disappointments that lie at the heart of angling. A kid learning to fish with an adult learns something absolutely priceless. He or she learns that I, myself, little ol' me, am okay, worthy, likable and lovable. As long as the adult does not demand that the child catch fish, catch a big fish, learn to cast in ten minutes, or push, pull, preach or insist on perfection, the child will probably come away feeling that, "Hey, I must be okay. Dad likes to be with me. Just ME!"

This is what self-esteem is all about: liking me for being me, for having my own thoughts and feelings and wishes and dreams and knowing, deep down, that this is not just okay, but wonderful and *the way it should be*. A kid who loves his life and the people in it isn't very likely to ruin it with drugs or booze.

Now then, I think there might be a big walleye just off that point over yonder. You ready?

Building Self-Esteem

There is a little trick to building self-esteem in young fishermen that every uncle, grandpa, parent and helpful adult ought to know. To help a kid get these good, self-esteem feelings, you must learn to bite your tongue just hard enough to avoid being overly critical or judgmental. If you ever take a kid fishing, something I cannot recommend too strongly, here's how to build self-esteem with the tongue-biting technique.

Father: "I see you just broke that expensive rod I bought you."
Son: "Yeah. Sorry. I guess I didn't know my own strength."

Father: "I wish you hadn't broken it, but we can always get another one."

The adult is unhappy about the broken rod, but doesn't go on to break the kid. Had this same conversation taken place between a critically judgmental father and his son, it might have gone like this:

Father: "I see you just broke that expensive rod I bought you."

Son: "Yeah. Sorry. I guess I didn't know my own strength."

Father: "Well, you should have! How could you have been so stupid!? If you would have only asked me, I could have got the lure free and you wouldn't have ruined my day! Honestly, when are you going to grow up!?"

Coulda, woulda, shoulda. These are the words of critical and useless judgment that kill off self-esteem. What's a kid to do, hit reverse and do it right on the rerun?

The latter father's focus is on the boy's failing as a person, not on his one-time mistake and poor judgment about rod strength. By leveling his disapproval on who the boy *is*, rather than what he *did*, the father manages to damage the boy's self-esteem and, as part of the bargain, the chance that the lad will ever want to go fishing again, at least with him.

Better to spare the boy who spoiled the rod.

Sorry. I just couldn't help myself. Here, let me get you a fresh nightcrawler.

A basic lesson in building self-esteem and raising happy fisher folk can be learned by answering one simple question. Which criticism would you rather hear: "That was a stupid thing to do," or "You're stupid"?

The first is a shot at something you can try to get right next time. The second is a blow to who you are. The difference in psychological consequences is staggering.

I can't tell you how many rods my kids broke or props they ruined hitting submerged rocks with my boat motors. I can't tell you how many times they lost valuable tackle, or dulled my favorite fishing knives sawing firewood, or left bird's nest in my spinning reels, or didn't replace the boat gas and enabled me to run out of fuel three miles out. In fact, when they were teenagers and fishing on their own, my standard question to them when they came back from the lake with my boat and gear was, "What's the damage report?"

I didn't like what I heard sometimes, but I came to accept that making mistakes is in every kid's job description. Not just a few mistakes either, but plenty, and sometimes expensive ones. When you accept this, your life as a parent will smooth out like a bass pond when the wind dies.

Kids don't come with perfect judgment or very much common sense. Common sense comes later, sometimes much, much later. Kids do come ready to risk and ready to love. Be happy and thankful when they come home in one piece. They're still *coming home*.

The Fishaholism Payoff

Teaching a kid to fish and to love the out-of-doors, the waters, the birds and the intrinsic role of nature in our lives, instilling a life-long, pleasure-seeking habit, so far as I can tell, has no downside consequences except the cost of graphite rods and the odd bass boat. If addiction to drugs and booze are negative habits because they eventually destroy the mind, body, family and spirit, fishing must be a positive habit because it builds and strengthens these same things.

Habits, as the philosopher William James once said, "are the fly-wheels of our lives."

I've got plenty of bad habits, but fishing isn't one of them. I suppose I'm a fishaholic. I'm not ashamed to say it. If, as some theorists have argued, addiction is not so much a disease as it is a failed quest for wholeness and happiness, then fishing has worked nothing less than a miracle for me and those like me.

I see a good drop-off just up the river, so let me finish up.

It has never bothered me to own up to the fact that I am a pleasure-seeking creature. Seek pleasure, avoid pain. It's a dictum as old as the Greeks and as new as next week's neurosciences. Pleasure seeking is built into our genes, body and mind. We all like to get high, get a rush, get that rare and wonderful lift that comes from experiencing life at its most joyous, throbbing and sparkling best. Peaks of great happiness are reached by too few people. Fishermen get to go there all the time. Otherwise, how do you account for all those smiles?

I feel sorry for anyone who thinks getting high on life means sticking something up his nose or into his arm. If I could wish something true for everyone who uses this cheap trick to pretend life is good, it would be that they could, just once, get a chance to enjoy the freedom of being clean and sober and the serenity of lying on a riverbank on a warm summer afternoon in the company of a good pal, watching for a bobber to dive out of sight.

Some things have got to be believed to be seen.

— Ralph Hodgson

Luck and the Case of the
Smoking Smallmouth Fishermen

Many springs ago, my pal Larry Grande and I drove to the Snake River above Lewiston, Idaho, for an afternoon of smallmouth bass fishing. Neither of us had any experience with smallies but we gleaned what information we could from local sources, loaded up on night crawlers, No. 6 snelled hooks and bobbers, and found a slackwater slough where, we were told, there would be bronzebacks aplenty.

Larry, a mycology major from Penn State, took over the show. He explained that smallmouth were no smarter than yellow perch and, after guessing how deep the crawler should hang below the bobber, heaved his rig out into the slough. I copied his setup exactly and cast my hopes upon the waters. We held the rods for a time, but, after it appeared smallmouth bass fishing was slow business, we cut a couple of forked willow sticks and propped our rods up, catfish style.

Time passed. No bobbers dived.

More time passed. Still no bobbers dived.

Even *more* time passed. Nothing. We reeled in, checked the worms and made an adjustment for depth. He went deeper, I went shallower, and again we cast the rigs out.

Still Life with Fishing Bobbers.

"I think I'll have a cigarette," said Larry. "Maybe that will bring me luck."

Able to launch lectures on the slightest provocation, I told Larry we had been studying superstition in a learning seminar and asked if he would like to hear all about the psychology of luck and superstitious behavior.

"No," said Larry, "I want to catch a bass." He pulled his little silver lighter from his shirt pocket and lit a Marlboro.

No sooner had Larry taken his first drag than his bobber disappeared. Jabbing the cigarette between his lips, he grabbed his rod, set the hook, and started cranking. After several whoops and hollers and an astonishingly good fight by the fish, a very nice two-pound small-mouth lay at our feet. Larry killed it with a length of driftwood and we got right back to fishing.

The bobbers did not bob.

Time passed, but no fish struck. Then I decided to have a cigarette. As I lit the smoke, Larry shouted, "Your bobber! Your bobber! Fish on!"

I dove for my rod, reared back, and the fight was on. When it was over, another almost-two-pound bass was ours.

Things calmed down and we patted each other on the back. Dragging another volunteer from the coffee can, I slipped the hook through the worm's collar and set him out to do some serious bass work.

Time ticked by without a take. Five minutes passed. Then ten. Larry looked at me. I looked at Larry. Simultaneously, we both grinned. "Got a light?"

The rest is fishing history. It's not exactly memorable fishing history, but fishing history all the same. Larry and I smoked every cigarette we had and eventually caught our limits of smallies. As a consequence, it probably took us an extra 10 years to give up smoking. And, on those fishing days when nothing is working, I still find myself reaching around for a pack of coffin nails.

Superstition and Fishing

The most rational of mammals sometimes believe the most irrational things. Some fishermen will only wear their "lucky" hat, others become depressed when they lose their "magic" lure, and still others persist in spitting on their hooks. To the extent that a creature is capable of learning, it can fall victim to something we psychologists call superstitious behavior.

Spitting on your hook, a superstition my father introduced me to, ranks right up there with not walking under ladders, avoiding black cats, being careful on Friday the 13th, tossing spilled salt over your shoulder and knocking on wood after tempting the gods with a prideful statement. Lighting cigarettes to catch smallmouth is no different from these more classic examples, except that the former are taught to us by our culture.

All cultures have an established baseline for magical beliefs. Millions of rabbits have lost their feet to the popular belief that carrying a rabbit's foot brings good luck. You can still buy a key-chain bunny's paw in dime stores today. I have even seen a bunny-foot bass plug sporting a treble hook.

Of the folks who carry a rabbit's foot in the hope it *might* bring them good luck, *only those people who actually experience something positive* are going to make a habit of carrying a rabbit's foot around with them. If you bought a rabbit's foot on Friday to enhance your luck on a lottery ticket, crashed your car on Saturday, lost a huge muskie on Sunday, your dog died on Monday and you didn't win the lottery, chances are you will toss the rabbit's foot away and write the whole business off to silly superstition.

If you bought the rabbit's foot on Friday, just missed a crash on Saturday, caught a world-record muskie on Sunday, your dog came home after being lost for three days on Monday *and* you won the lottery, what then? You'd probably personally slaughter a couple of hundred bunnies, have their feet attached to gold chains and never leave home without one.

Is a lucky fishing hat any different? I think not. If the darned thing works, wear it.

Fishing is always a chancy affair and fishermen are especially prone to develop superstitious behaviors and beliefs. Almost all anglers get a shove down the curious road to superstitious fishing with the suggestion that they spit on their hooks for good luck, but only a few become slaves to the practice. And the smarter they are, the harder they fall.

On Becoming Superstitious

For those like my pal Larry, who would rather skip the lecture and catch fish, or think it's bad luck to know how some things work, it's a good time to flip to the next chapter — otherwise you're going to get the lecture Larry missed.

To learn a superstitious behavior, like lighting cigarettes to catch bass, two things have to be in place: a reinforcer capable of increasing the rate of a given response, and a temporal relationship between that reinforcer and given response; in other words, two things happening at the same time in the same place.

In the case of the Smoking Smallmouth Fishermen, the reinforcer was a striking fish, while the response that "triggered" the strike was lighting a cigarette. The temporal relationship between these two unconnected events was the elapsed time between lighting the cigarette and the strike of the fish, a matter of only a couple of seconds.

According to the laws of learning, the shorter the elapsed time between a given response and the positive reinforcer that follows it, the more likely the organism will learn this association and increase that behavior by repeating the response. The more associations, the stronger the response, or habit. Learning works the same way when the reinforcer is negative.

Anyone who has ever scolded a puppy for peeing on the carpet knows the scolding has to be done *right now* or your efforts comes to no good end. Humans are no different. Punish pronto or the punishment is wasted.

All living organisms learn the same way, even the ones with the fancy brains, which is why quick positive reinforcement is the breakfast of champions, and why quick negative reinforcement is the reason we only touch a hot stove once.

Schedules of Reinforcement

Larry and I persisted in smoking cigarettes to catch bass even after the system stopped working. To understand why, you need to get a handle on the concept of intermittent reinforcement. This fundamental learning phenomenon helps explain the existence of gambling Meccas like Atlantic City and Las Vegas, and why lucky old fishing vests are never thrown out.

To keep from boring you to tears, which the professor who taught me this stuff specialized in, let me just say there are all sorts of intermittent schedules of reinforcement, including fixed-ratio, variable-interval, and fixed-intervals, but the one that makes a hard-core fisherman out of you is the old V-R schedule: variable ratio. This is a training procedure in which reinforcement occurs only *some of the time*.

Harvard's Dr. B. F. Skinner, world-famous psychologist, noted this phenomenon. "Variable" stands for the irregular occurrence of the reinforcer, in the case of fishermen, striking fish. "Ratio" stands for casting. In a variable-ratio schedule the poor fisherman can never predict the next strike, but knows that in order to draw the next strike *he must keep casting*. He could get a strike on the 20th cast, the 59th cast or the very next cast. One thing is sure. You can't catch a fish without casting.

In the days when I imagined myself in a white coat conducting important bench-type research on lower organisms like college sophomores, I trained a pigeon to peck a disk for a pellet of pigeon food. You can teach a hungry pigeon to peck a disk to get one pellet, then teach it to peck three times to get a pellet, then give it a pellet after seven pecks, then 11 and then, just to be nasty, pay the little bugger off any old time it strikes you.

Before you know it, and as long as the pigeon is hungry, the poor thing will bang away at the disk practically forever to get that next pellet of pigeon food. Nothing produces a persistent pigeon like a V-R schedule. And if you stand back just a bit from the bird and let your eyes defocus, you can see a steelhead fisherman standing waste deep in an icy river, casting, casting, casting, casting, casting practically forever.

Resistance to Extinction and the Die-Hard Angler

The persistent behavior of a fisherman and his unwillingness to quit casting is called "resistance to extinction." This simply means a given habit is strong. As an example of how powerful superstitious habits can become, I once came upon a small, angry fisherman sitting on a dock staring at the angleworm on his hook as if it had sassed him.

"What's the matter?" I asked the boy. "You look upset."

"I am," he growled. "I can't get this worm to work. I've spit on the hook, I've spit on the line, I've spit on the bobber and I'm going to spit on this worm till it works."

"So what are you doing now?" I asked.

Eyeing me as if I was born stupid, he snapped, "Waitin' for more spit."

The strength of any fishing habit, superstitious or not, depends on what sort of schedule of reinforcement was operating at the time the response was learned. The strength of the lad's habit could be measured scientifically, as Pavlov did with his dogs, by how much spit he produced. A habit like steelheading can be measured in how many casts, like pecks on the disk or pulls of the slot machine handle, the angler makes before finally giving up, or extinguishing.

Using my own pathology as an example of a variable-ratio schedule of reinforcement and the strength of habit it produced, the first time I went steelhead fishing, I made several hundred casts, and I caught two fish, on a V-R schedule.

Then I fished several days without a hit. Then I caught a 10-pounder. Several thousand casts later spread over the next few trips,

I caught a very nice 16-pound hen on a "magic" lure snagged from the bottom of the river on an earlier retrieve. The lure was a red-and-white Dardevle. After catching that nice ironhead, and unaffected by anything as irrational and goofy as superstition, I rushed right out and bought two dozen Dardevles.

I caught no more steelhead on Dardevles, or anything else, for a month. The season wore down. After thousands and thousands of more casts, I suddenly caught two Grande Ronde River steelies in two casts from the same pool.

I have never been quite the same since.

The next fall, the steelhead runs were poor. That did not discourage me. Like my hungry pigeon back at the lab, I kept right on responding. And, like any number of little old ladies in Las Vegas, I never knew which cast would bring the next strike. I responded at a very high rate, a rate of response so high it began to threaten my marriage.

I didn't count casts that fall, but I did keep track of how many trips I made to the river to earn that longed for, dreamed about, silver, slashing, hard-fighting reinforcer called a steelhead trout.

Would you believe I took ten trips without a strike? Fifteen? Twenty? How about twenty-six?

That's what it was, twenty-six trips without a bump! The guys who set the payout schedules for Las Vegas slot machines could have invented steelhead fishing.

My rate of responding for steelhead nearly extinguished, but occasionally the habit returns and, before I know it, there I am once again, casting, casting, casting, casting. Practically forever. And sometimes with a Dardevle.

Luck

You can now understand how powerful a connection might be made between the accidental convergence of rare events, like catching a trophy fish just as you are adjusting a new fishing hat. Imagine a brain starving to make sense out of nonsense, which is what some

people call fishing. Touch your hat; catch a trophy. The brain leaps
at the chance to connect the new hat with a great fish.

"Big fish!" the brain screams. "New hat. Good luck!"

Then, "Bigfish, luck, newhat!"

Then, "Luckfishhat!" followed by, "Lucky Fishing Hat!"

Trust me, I know how these neurological associations work. I have
a whole wall of lucky fishing hats to prove it.

This is not to say there is never a connection between superstition
and some real outcome. The belief that three on a match is bad luck
originated during the trench warfare of World War I. A sniper spying
the flash of a striking match took the time it took to light one cigarette to shoulder his rifle, two cigarettes to get on target, and three
cigarettes to get off the shot. Wearing garlic around the neck to ward
off disease began during the great plagues of the Middle Ages when
the crews who buried the dead wore garlands of garlic and drank
garlic-laced wine to fight off the stench of decaying bodies. We now
know that bubonic plague–carrying fleas hate garlic and will not suck
blood from such a smelly source. And neither will a vampire.

Regardless of how accidentally some fishing superstitions get
started, it is important to remember that some reinforcer must continue to follow the response if that response is to be maintained. This
reinforcer is generally catching more fish. As long you keep catching
fish, the lucky hat is working. If the lucky hat works reliably enough,
and long enough, and you can convince others of the powers of the
hat, you can probably open a lucky fishing hat business and make a
fortune.

You may also become a legendary fisherman. Even mythical.

As measured in human lifetimes, some fishing superstitions have
spanned generations. The boy on the dock spitting on his worm is a
recent example from our culture. In the islands of the South Pacific,
fishermen angling within the reef need not take any special pains to
go fishing. They just up and go. Small fish within the reef are generally easy to catch, but should an islander wish to venture beyond the
reef where the fish are bigger and things become more chancy, the

ancient fishing gods must be propitiated and rituals observed. The more there is at stake, the more likely superstition is to occur, which is why nobody believes in rainmakers until they're really thirsty.

Lots of curious stuff that goes on in this world is superstitious in nature. There are professional ballplayers who never change socks during winning streaks, horse racing fans who say it's bad luck to bet on leg-taped thoroughbreds, and fishermen who swear that if the cows are lying down the trout won't rise. This last one, by the way, is absolutely true.

Larry and I finally did unlearn the connection between cigarettes and smallmouth strikes. It took many years and, of course, there were other dark forces at work, like primary nicotine addiction and the fact that lighting a cigarette could also fire up a stalled mayfly hatch.

As I circle around and tie up the loose ends on this, I look back on the case of the Smoking Smallmouth Fishermen and am thankful that Larry didn't remove his hat and pluck a stray hair from his scalp just as that first bass struck.

Otherwise, I might be bald.

Nature is indifferent to our love,
but never unfaithful.

— **Edward Abbey**

The Incidental Cure

Sometimes by choice, but usually for reasons more obligatory, I spend a little time in places like New York City, Los Angeles, Tokyo or Paris. Except for early risers strolling through the inner recesses of Central Park just at dawn, the only people able to find peace and quiet in such human hives are those who can afford penthouse rents . . . and the dead.

There comes a time in every city when I've had my quota of culture, bright lights, midnight sirens and strange encounters with stranger people. Sooner, not later, I begin to pine for pine trees. Lord Byron said of spending time in pathless woods or on the lonely shore, "I love not man the less but nature more." After three weeks in a big city, I begin to envy the dead.

I was not engineered for city life; too many hard lines, sharp contrasts, rectilinear edges, stiff buildings, hard concrete, harder-to-know people, Muzak and, of course, too little fishing.

Even if you could catch fish in the heart of a city, as people do along Chicago's waterfront, something is missing. Something soft, quiet, rhythmic and natural. Something at once irregular, smooth and soothing.

A breeze rippling willow leaves?

The sound of water swirling beneath bending ferns?

A rock wren's call as the sun rises through the tules?

The smell of sweet Syringa blossoms?

All of these?

Whatever is raucous, dissonant, clanging and distracting in the city disappears in fishing country. Edges soften. Decibels decline. Colors blend into greens and golds, grays and browns and blacks, mottled hues so wonderfully wrought that deer or brook trout can disappear in plain view. Leaves flutter, grasses bend, trees sway, water glides and the world is at once still and vibrant.

Standing in a steam casting to his quarry, an angler may be totally focused on his fishing. The only thing of import is the coaxing of a fish to the hook, but something else is happening. Something is there with him; behind him, in front of him, around, above and beneath him. Call it nature's embrace, that soft context of leaf and sky, stone and water in which, if we pause to reflect upon our space and time, we feel a more natural fit. Like summer rain falling on a dry land, the effect of nature on the soul is nothing if not healing.

As our fisherman angles from pool to pool, something seeps down into the fiber of his consciousness — something good. This gentle embrace holds and soothes our angler, calms his blood, opens a window and gives him a chance to see himself as part of a larger whole. If he is lucky, he might not only catch a fish, but find himself. Even if he only catches fish, he partakes of the Incidental Cure; the cure that comes from rejoicing in natural places and doing natural things.

I am hardly the first to notice the beneficial effect of nature on mental health. The Roman poet Horace wrote 2,000 years ago of rural virtue and urban corruption. Jean-Jacques Rousseau, Sigmund Freud, Henry David Thoreau and John Muir observed that man-made environments are not all they're cracked up to be.

Jimmy Carter, one of my favorite fishing presidents, wrote in his book *An Outdoor Journal*, "I have never been happier, more exhilarated, at peace, rested, inspired, and aware of the grandeur of the universe and the greatness of God than when I find myself in a natural setting not much changed from the way He made it."

Why do people feel this way, and why does the feeling seem so universal?

E. O. Wilson, Pulitzer Prize winner, Harvard entomologist and father of sociobiology, makes a wonderfully reasoned, scientific, evolutionary case for why it is we humans feel the fit and finish of being one with the world when we are in natural settings, and maybe especially when we are fishing. He calls it "biophilia," love of life.

The opposite of biophilia is biophobia. Humans are only naturally phobic about a few, potentially life-threatening creatures: spiders, snakes, sharks and toothy mammals bigger and meaner than ourselves. Fishermen who were not afraid of poisonous spiders, snakes, sharks, lions and such left the gene pool under unfortunate circumstances. Once you are out of the gene pool, you stop giving at the office and life goes on quite nicely without you, sans your bad-judgment genes. The result is that the next generations of fishermen are a little smarter and, eventually, go on to invent things like a cure for snakebite, the bamboo fly rod, and neoprene waders.

The biophilia hypothesis suggests that because we humans evolved in natural, parklike savannahs where we excelled as hunters and fishers, we are innately drawn to the optimal, familiar beauty of natural, parklike environments. These are our ideal settings, the ancient home country for which we all yearn.

Such savannalike settings are typically high ground overlooking water, much sought after by those who can afford view lots or large country estates. The Black Hills of the Dakotas were sacred savannahs to the tribes who lived there. Landscape architects meticulously reconstruct the parks of our past in the form of everything from golf courses to backyard escapes. Madison Avenue ad men and women routinely set up photo shoots of the new model cars powering through open, rolling country. The buildings and monuments of the great capitals of the world have routinely been placed in such settings, and then tailor-scaped to resemble our ancient stomping grounds. Even our cemeteries are copies of the "old country" of our common African past.

Dr. Wilson's thesis explains rather nicely why rivers threading through broad valleys call to me and why, when Norman Maclean titled his classic *A River Runs Through It*, he didn't have to explain the "it."

The out-of-doors "feels" better than the in-of-doors, but does it follow that urban life is mean and harmful or that nature has healthful effects on mental well being? Intuition and prejudice are cheap and science is expensive, but there has been a little work done to try to answer this interesting question; a question of increasing concern to a planet whose entire biosphere is jeopardized and whose natural places are disappearing at a terrible speed.

A psychiatrist friend of mine recently researched and wrote a paper on this subject. Jeff asked me to help him edit his paper. I kindly agreed to do so on the stipulation that, when the time came, I could borrow generously from his work. He agreed, after I promised I would someday show him the roll cast. I'll share with you what we know, just now, about this connection of nature to mental health.

First, the Bad News

Several experts have ascribed detrimental effects on mental health to civilization and urban life. Antedating Horace, "Mental Paradise Lost" doctrine holds that due to the increasing urbanization of modern life, the quality of our mental health has deteriorated over time. In a word, people are believed to be crazier now than they were, say, 100 years ago.

More people means greater density, more cities, more stress, more conflict, more emotional trauma, more shoelaces breaking with no time left and more folks' trolleys flying off the track. If people are getting psychologically more healthy late in this 20th century, they are doing a good job of keeping it a secret.

I am hardly alone in my view on the effects of city life on sanity. A new legal defense has recently come into use to explain why otherwise normal urbanites rape, shoot, rob and kill each other. Lawyers defending those who commit inner-city crimes contend that day-to-day urban life can induce "urban psychosis" — post-traumatic stress disorder — a condition already recognized in Vietnam veterans, rape victims and battered spouses. Attorneys employing the defense argue, with some limited success thus far, that life in the city, in and of itself, is so stressful that some city dwellers should not be held entirely responsible for their crime and deserve innocent verdicts or at least lesser punishment.

Does this mean rural-dwelling fishermen will be held to a higher legal standard? Are we, because we fish and spend time out of the city, more sane?

An attorney friend told me that defenses like "urban psychosis" take time to develop. English case law builds on itself, one case at a time, year after year. He also reminded me that wacky defenses like these inspire such inquiries as "What's the difference between a catfish and a lawyer?"

Answer: "One is a scum-sucking bottom-dweller, while the other is a fish."

What Does Science Say?

Several research studies associate adverse effects on mental health with airport traffic noise, noise in general, crowding, pollution, crime rates and the loss of the natural rhythms of day and night associated with things like shift work and jet lag. Comparisons between urban and rural living suggest that depression is twice as common in the cities. All over the world, urban areas report increasing incidents of clinical depression. Suicide rates are higher in first-world countries.

E. Fuller Torrey, in his *Schizophrenia and Civilization*, notes that the prognosis for recovery in people diagnosed with schizophrenia is better in developing countries than in the industrialized West. Does this suggest that the decrease in exposure to nature required by increasing industrialization not only makes people sicker, but keeps them that way longer?

If you have any bone knowledge, stuff you know automatically and down deep, the answer might be obvious. What you hear in the heart

of nature is harmony. What you hear in the heart of a city is disso-
nance. Fishing in natural places gives you the one at the cost of the
other.

This, by the way, is a good deal.

It doesn't take a federal research project to figure out that any time
you step out for an urban-brewed cup of coffee and run the risk of
being popped in a drive-by shooting, you're naturally going to experience higher levels of stress. Vigilance requires energy. If too much
vigilance is required, you become paranoid. Paranoia is the most expensive, demanding, physically and psychologically draining emotional state possible. A burglary here, a rape there, the neighborhood
grocer shot dead in his cabbages and, pretty soon, you're living a
white-knuckle life behind bars you installed yourself.

There is also the less dramatic daily sensory assault on your eyes,
ears, nose, throat, lungs and feet. These alone furrow the brow and
set the nerves on edge. And then there are the anonymity of city life,
the built-in estrangement and the odd chap who, as you pass along a
quiet thoroughfare, lunges out of a dark alley and shouts, "Fuck you!"

This is not the kind of psychological environment in which I feel
calm, safe or, for that matter, particularly sane. As I said, three weeks
in a city and I'm dead meat.

But, can nature really heal us?

Perhaps.

The nature-as-healthy theme is oft-repeated by philosophers, poets,
naturalists and, more recently, environmentalists, but psychologists,
psychiatrists, health and mental health experts, with a few notable ex-
ceptions, have been slow to recognize any potential cures that might
lie at the tail of a good trout pool.

This has not always been so. In the early part of this century, the
20th, it was widely believed that nature could restore troubled souls.
Thoreau said "in wildness is the preservation of the world." Early psy-
chiatric institutions were located in pastoral settings. Built to provide
respite and relief from the stresses and strains and increasing demands
of modern life, these hospitals were called "asylums" and "retreats."

The 18th century pythogenic theory of vapors implied that clean air was essential to the restoration of mental and physical well being. "A move to the country would be good for you," the healer recommended. "Go to California," Eastern doctors of the 1920s and '30s said, "the sunshine will help." From the natural settings of Japan's Shinto shrines to the mountain spas of Europe, people the world over go back to nature to seek cures.

Camping therapy, older than the turn of the century, has persisted to the present day in such programs as Boy and Girl Scouts, Outward Bound and adventure tourism. Researchers report dramatic symptom improvement in people who participate in these programs, regardless of age. "Highly satisfying" is the way most folks rate such out-of-doors experiences, with or without catching fish. The journals of participants routinely reflect a positive emotional experience being in the woods and, at least for a time, partaking of the incidental cure.

Studies suggest that even a "view of nature" may be healing. Hospital patients with windows opening on nature enjoy quicker recoveries, shorter post-operative stays, and lower incidents of minor post-surgical complications. Prisoners, the truly fishing deprived, with windows to the out-of-doors are found in generally better health and have fewer sick calls. And, studies confirm that viewing natural scenery, as opposed to urban views, reduces physiological activity and lowers stress.

Another friend of mine is a research psychologist whose curiosity runs toward the relationship of stress, depression and the immune system. Dennis found that stress enhances the risk of becoming depressed, and that depression, once underway, suppresses T-cell counts. T-cells are those wonderful little killer cells that circulate through your blood and stomp out invading bugs — including viruses and those tumor-starting mutant cells that cause cancer. If, according to Dennis, you can avoid excessive stress, the odds are you won't get depressed. And, if you don't get depressed, you probably won't ever get too sick to go fishing.

Interesting research questions include, "Does time spent fishing in natural environments reduce stress and, thereby, provide a kind of inoculation against illness?"

"Does fighting a wild trout in a wild place empower one's immune system to fight off everything from colds to heart disease to cancer?"

"Does fishing, if you can get enough of it, increase one's general state of health and thereby prolong one's days upon the earth?"

Of course it does. Otherwise, the old Babylonian proverb that "The gods do not deduct from a man's allotted span the hours spent fishing" wouldn't be true. And, anyone with an IQ higher than his wading shoes knows this is true.

If someone like my friend Dennis wants to prove this thesis by spending long days and nights in his lab, that's okay. As for me, I'll spend those long days and nights out on the stream stretching leaders against rainbows and, with every cast, adding time to my life span.

A Final Thought

If nature and fishing in natural places are good for what ails us late in this 20th century, and can keep us healthy into the 21st, it seems to follow that the more pristine the natural setting, the better it ought to be for us. A week in the Bob Marshall Wilderness catching wild cutthroats ought to do us more good than a week fishing blues off the tip of Manhattan Island.

Likewise, rivers and streams that have been channeled, dammed and spanned by everything from bridges to power lines ought to jolt our nervous system, not calm it. A seascape studded with offshore oil derricks should stab our soul, not soothe it. And a lake made grotesque by the tumorous growth of high-rise condos along its shoreline should cause a clamor in the blood, not a sanguineous flow. Nature made unnatural by the hand of man does not lower my blood pressure, but raises it.

A single Styrofoam cup found floating on the surface of a trout pool causes my jaw to set and my molars to grind. If I find a blue-winged teal dead, entangled in a coil of monofilament line, or spot a beer can winking up at me through slick green water, I, too, feel myself slip sideways toward the kind of rage that sponsors everything from heart disease to drive-by shootings. Any degradation of nature we can sense in whatever way we come to know that something is no longer as it was before being "improved upon" moves us away from peace, and toward insanity.

If man has not yet reached escape velocity from his psycho-evolutionary past (we are, until proven otherwise, a fairly basic, bipedal, overly self-conscious primate with lower back pain) then it seems to me that we had better take even better care of the places where the fishes live. Because if it turns out that our mental instability is somehow the result of our destruction of nature, then our future as a species might be a good deal more dreary than any of us has yet imagined.

Mind you, I enjoy the accoutrements of modern life: freeways, pickup trucks, VCRs, fast food and three-weight graphite fly rods. But, if I become unmindful of the important things, of the places from which I came, and the places to which I am drawn, the cost of civilization may become too dear.

The incidental cure, then, is simple: angle often, in natural places, and work to keep those places natural. It's the kind of medicine I can take.

To fish or cut bait ... that is the question.

— the author

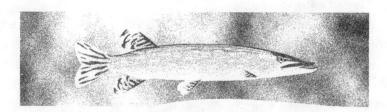

The Existential Angler

On a warm spring day in 1980, my middle son and I were fly-fishing for rainbow trout on the small, out-of-the-way stream in eastern Washington State where I found the grass pickerel and the notion for this book began. (Out of love for this particular corner of the cosmos, I will leave its location a mystery.) The larks were singing, the trout were rising and, as Sunday mornings in May can go, this one was perfect. "Was," that is, until the end of the world began.

Standing at the head of a large pool, the boy and I studied a sinister black cloud far to the west.

"What is that?" asked the lad.

"Don't know," I said, tying on a No. 12 Adams. "But it looks pretty dark for a storm cloud."

"And big," said the boy, with a touch of alarm in his voice.

Looking up after daubing a little floatant on my fly, I noticed the black cloud had suddenly doubled in size.

"Odd," I thought, laying out a cast. "I wonder if that's the end of the world."

Until he sees the end of the world coming, a fisherman never really knows of what sort of stuff he is made. He can be a decent, hard-working, honest family man whose only wish is to get along with others while he tries to get in as much fishing as he can, but present him with the end of the world and, suddenly, he will be obliged to wrestle with such profound questions as, "If there is life after death, will I need waders?"

For the angler suddenly presented with his own mortality, there are only five ultimate, existential concerns: death, freedom, purpose, meaninglessness and lure selection.

I have dealt with free choice and lure selection elsewhere in this text, so I will now tackle the remaining issues.

Considering these issues often creates what we psychologists call an "existential crisis," which is nothing more than plunging into that dark pit of doubt and angst where the existentially aware angler must grapple with such questions as his or her own death. He has to look deep into the mirror and ask the ultimate question.

"Do I fish . . . or cut bait?"

Fishing seems to bring the angler closer to philosophy and the deeper questions. While fishing you are closer to the great wheel of life and death, life following death, death following life.

While standing in a stream in late summer perhaps a fourth of all the organic things surrounding the angler are dead or dying. Great trees lie rotting in the sun. Bleached deer bones rest in the dark timber. A small trout is taken downstream by a kingfisher. The fall colors are showing. In such settings it is hard to deny your own mortality.

For every truly religious fisherman who has never doubted the existence of God, and has thereby secured the necessary guarantees for a pleasant afterlife, there are many more stuck with the ordinary fears of mortals. Because our faith is imperfect, we are likely to experience at least one existential crisis during a lifetime. Some folks only tumble into this black psychological hole on the heels of a near-death experience or after receiving a terminal diagnosis. Others struggle with things like death, freedom, purpose and meaninglessness almost every time they go fishing, philosophy being a favorite campfire subject.

I have a pretty good existential crisis about once a month — usually when I'm driving east into town toward my consulting office, instead of west to my favorite trout stream.

"What is man's purpose?"

"What is his place in the cosmos?"

"What happens after death?"

"Why do the big ones always get away?"

There are no correct or knowable answers to most existential questions. Their purpose is not so much to solve the imponderable mysteries, but rather to give each of us an intellectual arena in which to pursue self-knowledge while we wrestle a few of our fears to the ground.

Facing one's fears is not only the hardest thing any of us ever does, but it is also the most compelling of human tasks. It requires courage, determination and nothing less than a search for one's soul. The rewards are elusive and sometimes costly. But the endeavor can lead to the greatest prize of all: personal freedom, including the freedom to fish without fear.

The boy took a nice rainbow, cradled it in the water for a photo, and then released it. It was his sixth fish. I had caught none. We looked up to check on the approaching end of the world, now a huge black cloud stretching across the entire western horizon. It struck me that if the end of the world was approaching, I needed to get a hookup fairly soon.

My scholarship into existential philosophy and psychology permits me to take only a shallow wade into the difficult and wrenching questions asked by the giants of philosophical thought. Still, I believe that until a fisherman struggles with death and courage and meaninglessness, he will be haunted, knowing deep down that he is only 87 cents worth of cheap chemicals waiting to dissemble. Without a personal philosophy and absent the ability to master our fear of death, we will not live life to the fullest, nor be all the fishermen we can be.

We need to make what sense of such things as death and fishing as we can.

First, we all fear death, or at least having to die to get there. We tell others we don't fear death, but after midnight, alone in the still, wee hours, no one really wants to die. Even acutely suicidal people want to live, if only they can find a way.

As a suicide expert, I spend a lot of time with people who want to die, or who have already tried to kill themselves because life seems to them utterly hopeless and futile. Depressed and desperate, suicidal people wish to stop living not to end their existence, but to end the *pain* of their existence. Except in rare cases, suicide is an escape from, not a solution to, the problems of living.

Failed suicide attempts land people in nursing homes and wheelchairs, scarred and brain-damaged. For those without perfect faith, there is the possibility that killing yourself lands you in a state of non-existence, an utter, immutable nothingness, where, after you are pronounced dead as a door nail, you need never worry about dull hooks again. Or anything else. Forever and ever.

To come to terms with yourself, I suggest you think a little about your impending death and feel a little anxiety. It is a good thing to think about your death. No one else is going to give your death as much attention as you will.

This is not morbid. This is necessary. Thinking about death helps keep your priorities straight. It might even put a kick in your casting.

The black cloud now stretched along the horizon from north to south. It was moving toward us fast and had begun to blot out the sun, causing a soft, weird darkness to fall upon the trout stream. The birds, apparently perplexed, stopped singing, and a spooky hush filled the meadow. Remembering biblical passages from my youth, I couldn't recall darkness at midday ever heralding good news . . . though the drop in barometric pressure might trigger a huge mayfly hatch.

I asked the boy, "What do you think?"

"I think we should get the hell out of here. That's not a normal cloud."

Have you ever noticed how the guy who's been catching all the fish is the first one to say "Let's go home" when a spot of bad weather shows up?

"Hummm," I said. The Hanford Nuclear Reactor was less than 100 miles southwest of our trout stream. From the direction the cloud was approaching, if something had blown up down there like everyone kept saying it would, it just might have contained enough killer stuff to put us down for the count.

"Just let me hit this next pool," I said to the boy. "I really need to catch at least one fish."

Life and death are interdependent. You can't have one without the other. To fish fully, we must fish in the face of death. This is good, not bad. To relish life means to know and to feel that it is always ending; not just for others, but for ourselves, too. And, though life ends here, it begins there, for someone or something else. Life may not end tomorrow, but surely, it will, and sometimes sooner than we think. It is this awareness of life following death that lends a wonderful, bittersweet taste to a perfect day on a perfect stream, and gives authenticity to our angling.

Without this gnawing knowledge of our own mortality and the insight that our lives are escaping even as we live them, the fish I catch today have little meaning. Once we know for certain that there will surely be a last tomorrow, a last cast and a last fish, we can stop putting off joy and dig in, now, with both hands.

The Zulus have a saying. "The future is not coming toward you, it is running away. So you must chase it."

Some of my suicidal clients have been fishermen. *Have* been. They say they will go fishing again as soon as they find the time, or when they get a boat, or when the weather is better, or after the house is painted, or if someone asks them to go. Preoccupied with the mundane and overengaged in idle chatter, they spend the only life they have on everyday chores and ordinary diversions. Unmindful that life is always pinching out, they piddle away their days in a darkening depression.

They react to the requirements of existence, rather than act on the richness of life. They are passive, reluctant and keep their excuses at the ready. For some, giving up fishing equated to giving up life itself. Part of the cure for depressed anglers is, of course, to limber up the rod and start to live again. Because hope is cast for and retrieved, the act of angling itself is life-affirming. I, for one, don't want to get down to that day when I need only one more clean shirt and have to say, "Damn. I should have gone fishing when I had the time."

People who have tested death or know they are dying in the near term, which are the only times death seems to get our attention, often come to realize that things like pride, money, status, material success, big homes and fast cars don't amount to squat. What does are not the trivialities that consume us, but golden poppies nodding in a spring breeze, blue skies, Christmas carols, a child's smile, holding a puppy, hugging loved ones, falling snow and raindrops dimpling a hidden brookie pond in a deep wood.

It was pretty obvious that the black cloud was going to kill us, especially when a heavy, sootlike material, which I assumed would tick like crazy under a Geiger counter, began to fall from the sky. It settled on the petals of the bluebells in the meadow, turning them a deathly, ashen gray. My son, always a bright boy, said, "Let's get the hell out of this!"

"Just one trout," I said, calmly, "before it gets too dark to see."

"Too dark!? Geeze, Dad, we're being buried alive by this stuff! Are you ready to go?"

I didn't answer. I was thinking we were probably already fried and that, in case there's no fishing on the Other Side, if there is an Other Side, I'd better get in one last good trout before passing over. If there is a Hell on the Other Side, and assuming I am going Down instead of Up, which those who know me well think a reasonable probability, they might put me on a perfectly beautiful stream loaded with trout and then not let me catch any.

I made another cast and watched for a rise.

There are people who have survived their suicidal jumps from San

Francisco's Golden Gate Bridge, though over 1,000 have been killed by the leap. Most everyone who takes the big plunge dies, and it's wrenching to think about their last moments, especially when you interview the survivors who, to a man and woman, say things like, "No sooner had I cleared the railing than I knew this was a bad idea." Or, "I shouldn't have done this." One woman survivor heard the words *"I want to live!"* screaming in her ears the whole way down.

After the jump and rescue, all the survivors interviewed gained new insight into the meaning of life and their personal part in the drama. Some felt closer to their concept of God. Some felt a wonderful benevolence in the world. All experienced a new awareness of the miracle of life, and a new oneness with that life.

If you are ever ambivalent about whether or not to go fishing, you might remember these special people. Their existential crisis behind them, none went on to commit suicide.

Purpose, Choice, Freedom and Meaninglessness

It is probably not enough to simply accept death, quit your job and go fishing for the rest of your life, though considering some of the excuses for a so-called meaningful existence I've seen, there are certainly worse ideas. To my way of thinking, there is a bit more to it. Quite a bit.

I think we should leave something on the table.

I've found in my work with suicidal and dying people that it is very important to most of them to leave a little something on the table of life — a poem, a drawing, a stamp collection for a grandson, a handmade quilt, a kindness to be remembered, an act or a deed or a book or an old split-bamboo rod, or, like Mr. Carnegie, a library here and there.

The "something on the table" is the legacy, the part of you that remains after you're gone. It is often the only mark you leave after having passed this way, so what you leave on the table gives meaning and purpose to why you bothered to have lived at all. Our children are part of the something on the table, but the range is limitless.

To give purpose and meaning to life means to make conscious and constant choices about the immediate present while simultaneously accepting, and sometimes defying, death.

I often think of Ernest Hemingway as someone who practiced the art of living well while spitting in death's eye . . . and then writing about it. He was a fisherman like me and fired my ambition to write with his short story "A Big, Two-Hearted River."

You may not admire his male swaggering, but he lived what life he had fully, making no apologies to anyone. As a result of his uncontested decisions, and his taking full responsibility for his life and work, he left a great deal on the table for the rest of us, including one of the world's great fishing stories in *The Old Man and the Sea*.

Ernest Hemingway took his own life. You may think a suicide a coward, but only if you have never experienced the kind of endless mental torture the seriously depressed sometimes suffer. Like many great writers, artists and others touched with genius, Hemingway surely suffered from a classic mood disorder, a neurochemical dysfunction in his brain that brought on repeated bouts of debilitating depression. With none of the miracle drugs now available that might have put him right again, his mental anguish and exquisite psychological pain proved a greater foe than any he had ever faced. He had been to the doctors; hope for a cure was finally lost.

When you think about Mr. Hemingway and how he detested ordinariness, it makes sense that as a fisherman and writer his character Santiago would do what any angler worthy of his true purpose might do when faced with his own approaching death: go out alone in search of a great fish. You cannot start a story about the deeper meanings of life and death better than with the opening line, "He was an old man who fished alone in a skiff in the Gulf Stream and he had gone eighty-four days now without taking a fish."

Santiago would write his own last chapter.

I often ask my patients, "Who is writing the story of your life? And, if not you, then who?" It is not so important that we make something big and broad and lasting of our lives but that we own the possibility that we can. For the character Santiago, catching a big fish would do. For you, what? To fully accept authorship of the script we live is a first and necessary step down the path to psychological freedom, the freedom to love and work and fish.

Too often the answers to "Who's writing the script?" project authorship elsewhere.

"My wife."

"My husband."

"My job."

"My boss."

"My kids."

"My mother."

"The government."

Or all of the above. Any answer but "Me."

Psychologists call ducking personal responsibility "blame-avoidant rationalization," a fancy way of saying that it is easier to blame others for our failures and unhappiness than it is to look deep into that existential mirror and say "*I'm it*. I'm the one who chooses to do the things I do and to be the way I am."

This sort of introspection and acceptance of personal responsibility for one's life takes a grownup. And it's tough work, but where on your birth certificate does it say life is going to be easy? I like to remind my patients that though they don't cause all their problems, they have to solve them anyway.

The sooty stuff was blanketing everything and it had grown, to use a biblical adverb, exceedingly dark. I had yet to catch a trout. Finally, though, the boy prevailed.

"Now I know why Mother says you're crazy," he said. "You won' t go home skunked."

"That's true," I said. "I always figure there is one more cast in me and, therefore, possibly one more fish. Did I ever tell you about the friend of mine's father who died steelheading?"

"Tell me about it on the way home," said the boy, gently removing the rod from my hand.

After you have decided that your own death is both certain and sure, the hardest question in life is, "What do you want?"

This question frequently produces long silences. Many folks become immobilized by the confusion this inquiry produces, apparently undone by a query that requires an expression of the selfish self and a reordering of present values. Therefore, "What do you want?" is an excellent therapeutic question. If patients already have slick, well-reasoned answers to all the questions in the universe, why are they in a psychologist's office in the first place?

"What do you want?" cuts right through all the bull. It cuts through all the stupid, compulsive habit traps we are vulnerable to when we live our lives not making conscious personal choices on a daily basis. If we don't make them, those choices will be made for us . . . by others.

I am a proponent of enlightened self-interest. If you don't love you, and take care of your own life, who will? If you don't love your life enough to take charge of it, chances are you will end up too damn miserable to even be invited on a fishing trip. Who wants to be around someone who doesn't like himself very much, whose life is on hold, whose future is a sheaf of promissory notes?

Who wants to be around someone who, when you ask him if he wants to hike up a rough trail to a high and wild lake on the very good chance there won't be any trout in it anyway, whines, pees down both legs and wants you to make the decision for him so he can blame you later if the trip is a bust?

Outside of my consulting office, where I help folks repair malfunctions of personal responsibility, life is just too precious to fritter away on people unwilling to take their chances with the rest of us. As a pal of mine says when he calls in midwinter, cabin-fevered and ready to go fishing against all odds, "Let's do something, Paul, even if it's wrong."

Only humans can close their eyes and see themselves laid out in their best suit, toes up and cooling down. Each of us ought to share the burden and the joy of being the only sentient creature capable of knowing beforehand that it will surely die. Like the sound of a fish's skull as it receives the priest, there's a familiar thump when death hits the floor near us. We all know that sound. It's not a good sound or a bad sound, it's just the sound of one life ending as another begins somewhere out of earshot.

It's what we choose to do about the sound of our own death a-comin' that makes life and fishing interesting.

We can avoid the really big questions or we can choose to confront them. If we confront them, we are obliged to consider the meaning of our existence, its purpose, its absurdities, its truths as far as we can know them, and the breadth of our freedoms and the extent of our courage to choose among those freedoms. This is scary stuff, but may be the only way to find out who and what we are as human beings and come to live lives unencumbered by fear and trembling.

An old Spanish proverb says it all. "To live in fear is to live half a life."

To draw a full measure of the elixir of life, it helps to know that even if there are no final, or even reassuring, answers to the really big questions, at least we humans have the privilege to ask them. What other creature can live with the full knowledge that it has but a single life to live and decide to risk that in a deep wade through a swift river to get a little closer to a steadily rising trout?

I started the engine and flipped on the radio to learn that the end of the world was really not the end of the world after all, but the explosion of Mount St. Helens. We had pandemonium, but not nuclear pandemonium.

"Okay," said the boy, "tell me about your friend's father."

"Oh," I said, as the windshield wipers began brushing away the volcanic ash, "I hope I get to die like him. He had a good life and a good death."

"A *good* death?"

"The old fellow was a logger who cut wood for a living, but really lived to fish. He fished his whole life. When he was an old man and his wife died, he sold the family home and bought a cabin on a river somewhere along the Washington coast. He let the lawn go and wild blackberries soon overran the place. Living from his garden, he shot a grouse now and then, but mainly he lived to catch just one more big trout."

I turned on the headlights to pierce the dark and started down the ash-filled gravel road toward town.

"So how did he die?" asked the boy.

"He was fishing with a friend. It was raining and he hooked a huge steelhead. He fought it a long time before wading out to get the fish between him and the shore. In the fight, his bright yellow rain hat fell into the river and started toward the sea. With his rod arched high and the great silver fish flashing in the shallows, he waved to his friend and collapsed with a heart attack.

"His last words were, 'Get the net!'"

About the Author

A man with two careers, Paul Quinnett is both a freelance writer and a clinical psychologist. An award-winning journalist with over 500 stories, essays, and columns published in America's premier outdoor magazines, he has also written four books in psychology for the lay and professional reader. An expert on drug abuse, depression, and suicide, his best-selling *Suicide: The Forever Decision* has also been published in French, German, and Chinese.

His magazine writing credits include *Audubon, American Forests, Field & Stream, Sports Afield, Outdoor Life, Gray's Sporting Journal, the Flyfisher, Fly Rod & Reel,* and many others. Several of his stories have been anthologized. Currently fishing columnist for *Sporting Classics Magazine,* he's also published essays in such wide-ranging publications as *Newsweek,* the *New York Times,* and *Psychology Today.* His mentor and best-selling humorist, Patrick F. McManus, in a serious moment, once wrote "Paul Quinnett is one of the finest essayists writing today."

Pavlov's Trout: The Incompleat Psychology of Everyday Fishing was his first attempt to bring the two great loves of his life together. With essays on topics from the phenomenon of why fishermen lie to ethics to the neuropsychology of fly selection, the book has been predicted to become a fishing classic. The sequel, *Darwin's Bass*, is a further exploration of the psychology of fishing man. In his latest book, *Fishing Lessons*, he tackles the philosophy of fishing—a philosophy of enjoying life.

Heavily involved in training younger clinicians, he also serves as Clinical Assistant Professor in the Department of Psychiatry and Behavioral Science at the University of Washington School of Medicine. His specialities include couples counseling, stress management, and consultation to law enforcement agencies in the inland Northwest. He consults on fly-fishing for free.